Praise for *R*

'Breaking the rules has moved from being a risky thing to do to becoming a responsible thing to do. I have no doubt that positive, professional rule breaking is undoubtedly the next essential skill of the 21st century, and *Rule Breaker* is the definitive guidebook on how to it with the courage, ethics and imagination that could lead leaders to the breakthroughs we all need.'

SAM CONNIFF ALLENDE, AUTHOR OF *BE MORE PIRATE* AND CO-FOUNDER, LIVITY

'What a white-knuckle ride! Jackie Fast has created a book which leaves you breathless. This book demonstrates with precise clarity both why and how we can ditch the conventional wisdom which serves us no longer. The pace of change has been fierce in this new era, reaching a crescendo in 2020. As leaders, we need to be equal to that change. *Rule Breaker* is your roadmap to delivering that change. The stimulating combination of personal experience and real-life case studies gives clear direction on how we can all adopt a growth mindset, be rebellious, be more agile and lead by example. When you put this book down, you feel you are letting yourself down if you don't rush out immediately and make a difference. Truly inspirational and a must-read for all aspiring leaders in business, in public service, in society; in fact, in all walks of life. This book sets the leadership standard for at least the next decade.'

JOHN STAPLETON, THE AUTHENTIC ENTREPRENEUR, CO-FOUNDER OF NEW COVENT GARDEN SOUP CO AND LITTLE DISH

'Bedtime reading this is not. This book will get your mind racing and entrepreneurial spirit rising as it not only confirms what you had been thinking about the world in which we live and operate but gives practical advice on what you can actually do about it. There is no guide for those who innovate. Until now, that is. Jackie Fast gives real advice drawn from personal experience and subjective analysis to help you navigate a fast-paced and changing world. To break the rules, you need to know the rules. This book will help you decide which ones to break and which ones to make. No one can predict the future. No matter how brilliant at your job you may be. But you can prepare for a world in which everything has changed by knowing your own mind. Jackie Fast will help you clarify your thoughts, gain confidence and give you a chance to achieve your potential. And there aren't many books that can make that claim!'

JAMES MAX, TALKRADIO PRESENTER, *FINANCIAL TIMES* COLUMNIST AND BUSINESS ADVISER

'Full of brilliant zesty stories, this book is captivating to read and leaves you ready to take on the world.'

BRUCE DAISLEY, FORMER VICE PRESIDENT, TWITTER, AND BESTSELLING AUTHOR OF *THE JOY OF WORK*

'Jackie Fast is an essential analyst of what makes leadership work, disruption effective and rule breakers prevail. Nobody who wants to understand the way the modern world works should miss this book.'

MATTHEW D'ANCONA, EDITOR AND PARTNER, TORTOISE MEDIA

'Jackie Fast traces the new perspective on business structures and rules brought about by the internet, fostering a new breed of entrepreneurs and leaders. Well researched and enjoyable, this is a playbook for how to achieve success in the new era by inspiring the inner rebel in you to go their own way. A must-read for anyone looking to do things differently!'

CLAUDE LITTNER, PROFESSOR, ENTREPRENEUR AND ADVISER TO LORD SUGAR, *THE APPRENTICE* (UK)

'This is not only a fresh, unique perspective on leadership, it is the perspective on leadership we *need*. Jackie Fast's ability to recognize and convey what a modern leader is capable of leaves you nodding your head with an intense urge to underline every gem of information. Highly recommend!'
LAURYN EVARTS BOSSTICK, FOUNDER, THE SKINNY CONFIDENTIAL

'To be successful in the current climate, organizations need to be authentic. They need to have a point of view on the important topics affecting all of us. Why? Because people no longer want a transactional relationship with a company simply based on the buying of products and services; they want a more meaningful connection grounded in shared values and a purpose beyond profit. To make this transition, leaders must choose to do something different, something disruptive. In this thought-provoking book, Jackie Fast shows why the old rules need to be broken and how leaders can act now to build the type of organization their customers really want.'
JEFF DODDS, CHIEF OPERATING OFFICER, VIRGIN MEDIA

'Chuck the old rules out. Leaders of the future are forging their own paths. Who better to explain the new dynamics of leadership than Jackie Fast, embodying the spirit of a renegade maverick. As the world shifts, what counts now is your ability to bet on yourself, think outside of the box and courageously inspire others to come with you. Sharing a set of lessons learned, and creating a much-needed playbook now, Jackie Fast will bring out the brave leader in you.'
LISA WINNING, TECH ENTREPRENEUR

'There is far too little business journalism for business people. We've sadly settled for books about trading or "levelling up" or backwards-looking navel gazing. But Jackie Fast fixes the problem. *Rule Breaker* explores a seismic mind shift driving business in the 21st century, changing the way we think about business.

She offers a Rosetta Stone to help us key into the next era of innovation, technology and even the future of business.'
CORY JOHNSON, MANAGING MEMBER, EPISTROPHY CAPITAL

'Filled with insightful stories on how businesses of the future are defying a history of old management tactics that no longer work. If you are wanting to make an impact, put this on your required-reading list!'
YAO HUANG, FOUNDER, THE HATCHERY

'An exciting and valuable book on how, in these times of rapid changes, leaders must redefine their role and draw on different sets of skills to be able to face the future. The biggest risk a leader is facing today is in fact not the lack of skills, but a complacent attitude about skills previously acquired that no longer fit the present world. Therefore, being a rebellious leader is not the prerogative of a few outliers; it should become the mainstream thought on how to shape a vision and inspire for change. *Rule Breaker* fosters the kind of constructive debate and fresh thinking that breaks the status quo and will enable this new type of leaders to face the challenges ahead.'
MARINA TOGNETTI, FOUNDER AND CEO, MYNGLE

Rule Breaker

Rebellious leadership for the future of work

Jackie Fast

KoganPage

Publisher's note

Every possible effort has been made to ensure that the information contained in this book is accurate at the time of going to press, and the publishers and author cannot accept responsibility for any errors or omissions, however caused. No responsibility for loss or damage occasioned to any person acting, or refraining from action, as a result of the material in this publication can be accepted by the editor, the publisher or the author.

First published in Great Britain and the United States in 2021 by Kogan Page Limited

2nd Floor, 45 Gee Street
London
EC1V 3RS
United Kingdom
ww.koganpage.com

122 W 27th St, 10th Floor
New York, NY 10001
USA

4737/23 Ansari Road
Daryaganj
New Delhi 110002
India

Kogan Page books are printed on paper from sustainable forests.

ISBNs

Hardback   978 1 78966 769 1
Paperback   978 1 78966 767 7
Ebook   978 1 78966 768 4

British Library Cataloguing-in-Publication Data

A CIP record for this book is available from the British Library.

Library of Congress Cataloging-in-Publication Data

Names: Fast, Jackie, author.
Title: Rule breaker : rebellious leadership for the future of work / Jackie Fast.
Description: 1 Edition. | New York : Kogan Page Inc, 2021. | Includes bibliographical references and index.
Identifiers: LCCN 2020054188 (print) | LCCN 2020054189 (ebook) | ISBN 9781789667677 (paperback) | ISBN 9781789667691 (hardback) | ISBN 9781789667684 (ebook)
Subjects: LCSH: Leadership. | Creative ability in business. | Management–Technological innovations.
Classification: LCC HD57.7 .F377 2021 (print) | LCC HD57.7 (ebook) | DDC 658.4/092–dc23
LC record available at https://lccn.loc.gov/2020054188
LC ebook record available at https://lccn.loc.gov/2020054189

Typeset by Hong Kong FIVE Workshop, Hong Kong
Print production managed by Jellyfish
Printed and bound by CPI Group (UK) Ltd, Croydon CR0 4YY

For Hendrix Cash Huston who has changed my world for the better.

CONTENTS

Introduction 1

PART ONE
The Past 5

01 Business unusual 7
Becoming a leader 7
A new world needs new leadership 11
A rebellious leader is within us all 21

02 I built it in my bedroom 29
Necker Island, tech start-ups and the long journey back 29
The democratization of big business 34
It goes beyond influencer marketing 43

03 'Move fast and break things' is broken 51
The foundations of the internet were laced with LSD 51
Computers for evil 57
Greed is... gone? 73

PART TWO
The Present 79

04 Replacing the C-suite 81
Punk leadership drives the craft beer revolution 81
New managers become new leaders 85
The three core values of leadership 89

05 Earning the right to lead 105
    Are leaders born or bred? 105
    New rules to earn leadership 112

06 Complacency is not an option 133
    Embracing failure during my 15 minutes of fame 133
    Using data to avoid sandbagging 141
    Futureproof your skills and adapt to permanent change 145
    Goal setting in the context of evaluation 150

PART THREE
The future 155

07 The future is collaborative 157
    Defying all odds 157
    Partnerships required to change the world 162
    Playing with Fyre 169
    Collaborate for good 176

08 The future is here 181
    Rule breakers will create change 181
    Driving purpose through rebellious leadership 185
    Collaboration and shared ownership 191

Acknowledgements 197
References 199
Index 217

Introduction

The world is changing. But you already knew that.

You have likely spent countless hours reading and discussing how the world is changing. It is debated at the highest level in politics and played out on our screens during the 6 pm news hour. We are all obsessed with how the world is becoming vastly different from the world we used to know. But it is not the *how* part that you need to be preoccupied with. It is the *why* part of this shift that is particularly important to you. Why do so many diverse and distinct worldly events seem to have reached breaking point? Climate change, sexual harassment, gender and race inequality, global pandemics and democracy all seem to have arrived at a critical crossroads.

If the situation seems precarious, it is. And while momentum is beginning to drive a semblance of change, the reality is that it takes a new type of leadership to create the transformation to a better world we all long for.

Technology and social media have skewed our ability to clearly identify leadership for both better and for worse. We now see the flaws in leaders due to greater transparency in the media. We are disenchanted with the leaders we used to rely upon for inspiration. We are in desperate need for new leadership, new hope. And as our attention has shifted to our smartphones, so too has our search – inevitably leading us to our addictive social media feeds. However, the Insta-famous rise of influence has eroded our understanding of success and indeed true influence.

But you cannot deny the power of meaningful connections. For all the faults that lie with social media and digital technology, there are significant opportunities when using these platforms for new voices to be heard. It is this ability, these new voices, which are sparking positive change in the future of work.

As new leaders emerge in both work and life in general, one clear commonality they all have is that they broke all the rules. Rather than give in to the inertia of life confined by old playbooks, they have relied on instinct instead of sage advice to achieve the unachievable. While this may seem daunting, the truth is that by taking a slightly rebellious attitude towards everything you have grown to know about leadership it can be relatively easy to achieve the unachievable – but you must be willing to shift your mindset and do your homework. What will drive true change for the future is inspiration. And as everyone has the ability to inspire, this should instil hope in all of us during an era in which we have reached the tipping point on so many major movements.

It has become crystal clear that it is no longer acceptable to sit on the sidelines.

Therefore, the *why* part of this book is fundamental. To understand how to create a better future for yourself you need to understand why the previous rules of progress were created, and why they are no longer valid and need to be broken. You will learn that old rules propped up the few, while new rules prop up the many. Most importantly you will learn that being an inspirational leader in today's new world is inherent within each of us, provided you are equipped with the tools and a bit of confidence to break the rules.

Although there are many books that discuss rebelliousness as a route to success, they tend to imply that rebelliousness is an outlier concept among the masses of society. Branded a disruptor my whole life (the title of my *Forbes* profile in 2015 read 'Jackie Fast had to break the mould to make it'), I want to kill any notion that rule breaking is for the few. Instead I believe this new wave of rebelliousness is the beginning of what all leadership will become. It will guide the next revolution of positive change in both the world and in business and set the foundation for our future. Ultimately, I am asking you to be part of building that foundation.

This book is a culmination of personal experiences and curated case studies across diverse sectors to clearly illustrate how breaking all the rules is now fundamental to success in the future of work. We will review the quick rise of Kylie Cosmetics against the backlash of Amazon climate change walkouts and understand the failures of collaboration with Fyre Festival compared with the enormous success of Beats by Dre.

Having achieved significant success early on by going against the grain, I know first-hand the barriers to overcome. Fortunately, the tools needed are within everyone's grasp. I hope that by outlining this turning point and providing practical guidance to tap into your inner rebel, you too will be able to grasp them. These tools will enable you to become an exceptional leader in the future of work and inspire the world in the process – hopefully helping us all change our world for the better.

PART ONE

The Past

CHAPTER ONE

Business unusual

Becoming a leader

The green plastic seat was cold despite the bustle of the stamp collection exhibition going on around us. This specific event was my favourite among the hundreds of other exhibitions held in the commercial building in which our office was located in Central London. Although the 'Best of Italy' showcase was a treat with free food samples given out to attendees and office dwellers, there was something about the hum of hundreds of silver-haired hushed negotiators that resonated with me.

It was on this day, 11 February 2011, that I sat across from Mark Mylam. His experience was laid out between us on the pale orange Formica table which kept tilting when I put my elbows on it. I noted that the pieces of paper that contained his work experience were in pristine condition, surprising considering it had made the journey during the peak-hour jostle on the crowded London Underground. I had spent the previous evening wrapped up in my pyjamas in my bedroom pouring over Google searches in anticipation, ensuring I would ask the right questions. The trick it seemed was to ask situational questions: 'Tell me about a time you had to choose something else over doing a good job' and 'Tell me about a time you had to collaborate with a co-worker who was hard to please'. Quickly finding out Mark's previous full-time job was working as a ski instructor in Switzerland killed any hope of utilizing these questions effectively.

Not that I would have known a good answer from a bad one. This was the first time I had ever held an interview. Being only 26 years old, I had never hired or managed a single person in my entire short career. I desperately hoped Mark could not tell.

Mark was all smiles and genuinely seemed interested in the opportunity to come and work for me. He had an ease and friendliness about him that went beyond his 22 years of age and his excitement for wanting to work with me was infectious.

My business, Slingshot Sponsorship, was launched as a marketing consultancy, a way for me to pay the rent after I quit my job. It was set up without much ambition, just a run-of-the-mill one-man-band service that would help organizations and events find and secure new sponsors to add revenue to their bottom line. Having found moderate success in this area for my previous employer, which ran 52 annual events ranging from e-mail marketing breakfasts to summer socials, I took the chance to set off on my own with little clue about how to actually do so. But being my own boss sounded enticing. Much of what I gathered about starting a business I took directly from information online, largely from the UK government's website. It seemed relatively straightforward: get a business bank account and register your business. Two things that I managed to complete in less than four hours one evening after working my day job. And just like that, I was a business owner.

Considering the launch of my business took just a brief four hours of work, I was propelled into action with confidence.

Unsurprisingly, it turned out that making money from a business is considerably harder than setting one up. I would have loved to have hired an employee at launch, but without an office, even I understood that no self-respecting intern would be willing to work from home. After all, this was pre-pandemic and the value trade-off for internships was a chance to learn and gain experience which cannot be gleaned in isolation.

Looking back on that first year I recall much of it spent working in my pyjamas. I chased any potential opportunity and begged clients to work for them. It slowly started to pay off and eventually I had enough of what looked like an agency that I felt I could convince someone to join my ridiculously small team of one. Hiring an employee was a goal I had put in my original business plan as attainable after the first year. By my own estimation I was on schedule.

But the pressure of hiring my first employee was enormous. Having previously bounced around multiple jobs in both Canada and the United Kingdom, I had spent much of my formative career being wildly disappointed with both the actual work I was doing and the people I reported to. My combined lack of patience and outspoken nature meant I often did not last long. I vowed to never make the same mistakes if I ever became a leader myself.

I launched Slingshot Sponsorship in May 2010 from my rented room on an ex-council estate in London. Having been in the United Kingdom for a handful of years on an extraordinarily minimal salary, the furnishings were sparse and my only source of entertainment was a tiny television with terrestrial TV. I spent most of those early months stressed about paying my rent. My social life was non-existent. Instead my waking hours were spent hunched over my laptop propped up by pillows desperately searching online to try to utilize every marketing tactic to round up clients and generate revenue for my fledgling business. Every single invoice I raised, mostly for project-based sponsorship sales work, went into saving for my first employee. The money gradually accumulated in my business bank account until I had just enough to pay for one full-time salesperson's salary for a year.

Fully grasping how important generating clients was to be able to pay my rent, and the fact that much of the work involved pitching creative ideas to brands, hiring a full-time salesperson was the obvious next step. Unfortunately managing sales is tricky and hiring salespeople even more so. Unlike customer service, management, human resources and almost every other department in a business, finding out whether a salesperson is good or bad at their job at the beginning of their career is an impossible task. Salespeople need time to understand the product or service and cultivate leads. They then need even more time to close a deal. Being a salesperson myself I understood that if I was going to hire one, I needed to give them time to prove value to my business. I also understood that if I hired the wrong one I would see my entire savings wiped out waiting for results. A bad hiring choice would leave me broke and forced to go back into full-time employment in the corporate world. Or worse still, move back home with my parents in Canada.

Not only would this hurt financially, it would prove that I could not hack it as an entrepreneur – which would hurt my ego the most. I had invested a full year of my life doing everything I possibly could to make my business a success. Failure at this point was not an option. At that moment in time, it felt as if my whole future was riding on this one single hire.

Among HR professionals there is an ongoing debate between hiring on instinct or hiring on algorithms, with equation-based hiring being 25 per cent more effective.[1] However, in 2010 my access to algorithms was non-existent as was my hiring experience. Google only went so far, and I did not have anyone to ask. So, I went with the only thing at my immediate disposal, my gut instinct.

Among the crowd of Old Spice and Zimmer frames at the stamp collection convention, I hired Mark that afternoon. He accepted on the spot. And just like that, I became a leader for the first time in my life.

A new world needs new leadership

Our world is changing at a dramatic rate. As a society we are aware of this changing context because we see it during our everyday lives. We can curate our experiences through Netflix, have our groceries delivered to our door, and gain business advice from mentors across the globe in real time. However, much of what has been written about leadership remains embedded within old corporate structures of top-down management aimed to increase output through the assembly of people. Although work has moved on from the industrial revolution of factories, what remains is leadership and management tactics built on hierarchy and nepotism. Leaders who have created success on corporate structures that no longer exist in the same way. Leaders who go on to write best-selling how-to books designed to help you replicate their success by following the same guidelines. I am not saying these people are not great leaders; far from it. But great leaders of their time. Successful based on a different set of criteria from that which we are living through today.

This book looks at how great leaders come to be in *our time*. A time when selfies can build billion-dollar beauty brands and a car company's valuation exceeds that of a legacy automotive brand without having one physical dealership or car salesperson. These are extraordinary times. We are in a new world with no boundaries. What has not been possible historically is now possible. But it needs new leadership. New leaders with vision.

The first part of this book will outline the framework of change, crucially identifying a shift in global consciousness driven by technological advances. Over time, businesses are increasingly becoming less monopolistic, driven by advancements including streamlined processes, data organization and ease of communication. But what our common understanding of these business advancements rarely considers is how these achievements are underpinned by base human nature. This is compounded by numbers. There are more people who want their shot at the top and they are becoming increasingly more creative in achieving that reality.

It took 200,000 years for the world's population to reach one billion. The second billion was achieved just 130 years later in 1930, the third billion 30 years later in 1960, the fourth billion 14 years later in 1974 and the fifth billion in 1987. In 1970 alone (a year in which most of today's leadership authors started their careers), there were roughly half as many people in the world as there are now.[2] As with sport, competition in business drives advancement.

As this advancement continues, furthering life expectancy and quality of life, the fight for the top is compounded by those flooding the bottom. This will continue to accelerate, fundamentally changing how new leaders think and act.

Learning through patterns

As humans we curate our world through repetition and patterns. What has gone before is therefore likely to come after – a theory dating back to the time of hunters and gatherers. Which berries can be eaten without the risk of death? Who should go out hunting and where is there likely to be easy prey? How can you trust another person or tribe? The ability to sort and classify complex information is inherent in our DNA. We rely on this instinct as we try to achieve our goals – gathering the right information to lead us to the pathway to success. Often when success is not achieved, we believe that the fault lies in the information we have gathered. When we become stuck it is often due to not originally sorting information correctly. These failures are what props up the billion-dollar industry of shifting your mindset.

If you are willing to part with $945 you too can 'Stop settling for less... to become a stronger, more resourceful and more powerful person' by attending Tony Robbins' Unleash the Power Within seminar.[3] Robbins' techniques are based on neuro-linguistic programming (NLP), claiming there is a connection between neurological processes, language and behavioural patterns learned through experience. By changing your existing patterns through dramatic exercises such as walking on fire, Robbins hopes to significantly change your mindset to help you achieve your goals.

And changing your mindset is not just for the neophyte. Robbins' seminars are believed to have helped some of the most ambitious and successful people achieve greater. Famous actor Gerard Butler, known for action movies and stunts, is said to use Robbins' tactics in his everyday life to overcome fear – a state we wouldn't expect Butler to be worried about. 'Fear is a huge issue for me,' he has said. 'This technique Tony has is a really smart way to literally set those fears aside.'[4]

But what if what used to be hardwired is already being rewired? Not consciously through firewalks, but unconsciously – cultivated by the vast changes in information we now receive.

In the Stone Age, to prosper in a tribe, human beings needed to make judicious alliances. Who to share food with, who to hunt with and who could be trusted to return the favour. The ability to classify people in categories based on repetitions of patterns allowed individuals to make decisions faster on who could and could not be trusted, what leaders would bring you food and which would not. The faster you could make these decisions and identify these patterns, the more likely you were to survive.

Over time the information we gather has evolved the classifications we make decisions with. With so much information to sort in the Information Age, our classifications are becoming disjointed as we struggle to consciously identify the common patterns. Worse yet, the patterns that do emerge are often not reflections of the truth. This skewed viewpoint is caused in part by social media. Instead of recognizing patterns through our own experiences we now rely on other people's experiences shown through their social media feeds. Rightly or wrongly we use this to create our expectations. Therein lies the problem. The information we receive has become highly curated based on our appetite for consumption. Now more than ever we are familiar with overnight success and exceptions to the rule. By just clicking content that outlines how a high-school drop-out made millions you are primed to be served more content of this type. A pattern then begins to emerge which leads you to believe that dropping out of high school might not be the end of the world, but indeed the making of you. But this is far from the truth.

For example, the most popular occupation sought after in grade school is a career in professional sports; however, just 0.03 per cent of those who play basketball in high school ever go pro.[5] Despite the bleak statistics, millions of kids a year choose to focus on landing three pointers over doing their English literature homework, thinking they too are the exception to the rule. And it is this expectation to become the exception that is driving many of us to dig into our pockets for books, seminars and even firewalks to achieve overnight success.

The evolution of business structures towards innovation

Compounding the shift in work caused by our own hardwired classification patterns which are fraught with misinformation is the evolution of business structures. So, let us start at the beginning.

Corporate culture is said to have started in 1602 when the Dutch East India Company laid the foundation for how businesses operate today.[6] As the first company to ever list shares, it revolutionized business ownership, company valuations, speculative bubbles and stakeholder business drivers. At the height of Tulip Mania in 1637, the Dutch East India Company was worth $7.9 trillion – the equivalent of more than 20 times the value of the world's most important companies today.

FIGURE 1.1   The most valuable companies of all time

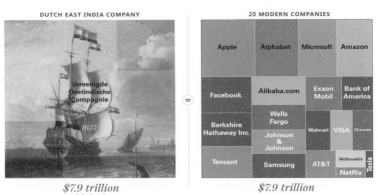

Reproduced with kind permission of Visual Capitalist (2020)

With a 21-year monopoly granted by the Dutch government for the spice trade in Asia, the Dutch East India Company had what everyone at the time sought after. This enabled them to push boundaries for profit, sending almost a million people to Asia, more than the rest of Europe combined. Commanding over 5,000 ships, many ships returned a profit to investors of 400 per cent and in the drive to increase profitability, many more ships were lost at sea. Not only did the Dutch East India Company transform the world, it also transformed the financial markets and its impact can still be felt to this day.

Innovations on the Amsterdam Stock Exchange such as futures contracts, options, short selling, and even the first bear raid (a stock market strategy where a trader attempts to force down the price of the stock by spreading negative rumours) were all driven by shareholders of the Dutch East India Company.[7] And the drive towards valuation for things we desire has not stopped for over 400 years, with the most recent initial public offering (IPO) of crude oil company Saudi Aramco reaching $2 trillion – officially emerging as the most valuable publicly traded company at its time of listing on 11 December 2019. With oil being the source of more than a third of the world's energy, it is unsurprising that Saudi Aramco's shares surged with a 10 per cent increase in share price on the first day of trading, even in the wake of Swedish environmental activist Greta Thunberg's impassioned speeches. Even the deadly coronavirus did little to impact the share price which briefly dipped in March 2020 as investors worried about global demand.

And while much has been debated regarding these monopolies, a disproportionate amount has been written about their leaders. This is common among some of the world's most impactful businesses and further outlines the skewed nature of leadership information we aim to assimilate.

Take Johan van Oldenbarnevelt who founded the Dutch East India Company. Not only did he single-handedly initiate and broker the deal amalgamating half a dozen companies that traded in the Far East into the Dutch East India Company in 1602, but a decade later he also created the model for joint stock ownership by shareholders. By most accounts these are two extraordinary achievements in a lifetime, and yet historical reports refer to his life through a political lens rather than highlighting his entrepreneurial savviness. What has been written of his business achievements links Oldenbarnevelt to the single idea, rather than his putting it into action. However, it was the *execution* over many years which later led to greater advancements for business that made his initial idea so successful.

Having a great idea has indeed made great men and is often utilized today to create an 'us and them' mentality within business recognition. It is often easier to attribute an individual's success to a good idea, a pattern that humans can spot as they understand what has come before and what will come afterwards. As most people are not privy to each individual business strategy, our understanding of what makes a business great, and therefore its leader great, is singular in nature.

It is therefore easy to compartmentalize entrepreneurial greatness as exceptional, as good ideas are exceedingly difficult to find; great ideas almost impossible; and true innovation seemingly unreachable. We stack our bed-side tables with business books helping us discover the next big idea. We continually search for tools that promise increased effectiveness. We obsess over communicating our ambitions and personal goals. It is why films about entrepreneurship were some of the most profitable movies in the decade between 2006 to 2016 with *Pursuit of Happiness* (2006) bringing in $307.1 million (budget of $55 million), *The Social Network* (2010) bringing in $224.9 million (budget of $40 million) and my personal favourite *The Wolf of Wall Street* (2013) bringing in a whopping $392 million (budget of $100 million). There is clearly a big appetite for those seeking greatness.

Even if we are not interested in becoming the next Steve Jobs, the link to becoming great through one big idea is constantly driven into our mindset. In business schools most educators stress the importance of launching a new business one of two ways: either with a brand new idea or a better solution to an old problem. Yet very few ideas are truly original. Many of today's leaders have not revolutionized industries by themselves. Rather, the revolutionary changes are the result of marginal gains the whole industry will have made over a longer period. These incremental gains are what take industries beyond their historically identified and self-proclaimed boundaries, often small steps over a long period of time.

It is not just in businesses that small steps can create radical success. Much has been written about Dave Brailsford and his extraordinary achievements with British Cycling using this concept of marginal gains. Brailsford states: 'The whole principle came from the idea that if you broke down everything you could think of that goes into riding a bike, and then improve it by 1 per cent, you will get a significant increase when you put them all together.'[8] His innovations were small adjustments, areas you would suspect would be common practice among professional cycling teams. They looked at the minute details from testing different massage gels on recovery, to redesigning the bike seats to make them more comfortable.[9] These seemingly small improvements radically changed the fate of the team and during the 10-year span from 2007 to 2017, British cyclists won 178 world championships and 66 Olympic or Paralympic gold medals – making them the team with the most successful run in cycling history.[10]

This approach is often underutilized in business, although its pattern emerges throughout history and can be seen with some of the most seemingly innovative companies and rebellious leaders of our time.

Hailing from the Netherlands and at the age of 35, Alfred Peet arrived in San Francisco, California in 1955 with big dreams. Having spent a lifetime enjoying exceptional hot drinks, beginning in childhood with a coffee roaster for a father, to his early career working as an apprentice at Twinings coffee and tea company in London, it was not lost on him that although the weather might be better in California, the coffee certainly was not. He opened his first shop, Peet's Coffee & Tea, in Berkeley, California on 1 April 1966.

In love with the craft of creating that perfect cup, Peet jumped at the opportunity to share his history and love of roasting with three university kids, Zev Siegl, Gordon Bowker and Jerry Baldwin, who were intrigued at what made Peet's Coffee so different. Three friends who later went on to launch the first Starbucks in 1971. But today, it is the Shultz name that has become synonymous with Starbucks. Ironically, New Yorker Howard Schultz did not first set foot in a Starbucks coffee shop until 1981, 10 years after it launched. He joined the company just one year later.

Schultz spent the first five years of his employment developing and executing the marketing strategy, but he struggled to gain internal buy-in with the three founders for his personal vision to turn Starbucks into a more Italian-feeling café experience. Through a twist of fate, the frustrated Schultz eventually acquired the six Starbucks stores in 1987. By 2020, Starbucks had over 23,000 storefronts in 75 countries and was on the list of the 100 most recognized brands in the world.

Although this is a significant achievement, it is important to recognize that Schultz did not reinvent the wheel. He did not even reinvent coffee. Instead he copied an idea older than the Dutch East India Company itself and created a coffee culture around espresso rather than the traditional American filtered cups of joe.

Schultz is often the first to admit that Starbucks' success does not lie in their coffee, but in the fact that he was able to create an experience. He defines his business as 'the business of human connection and humanity, creating communities in a third place between home and work'.[11] It is the little things that add into what makes an experience great, not necessarily the big idea to do so. After all, don't we all want great experiences?

Often cited as one of the world's leading rebel entrepreneurs, another big idea creator famous for innovation is Sir Richard Branson. But like Schultz, when you scratch beneath the surface the aforementioned innovation could just be understood as common sense. Let us look at Virgin Atlantic, known in the airline industry as an innovator. Launched in 1984, their innovations included injecting fun. Differing from their competitors, they utilized bright red uniforms and cheeky attitudes including advertisements with catchy slogans such as 'British Airways doesn't give a shiatsu'.

At their launch, innovation was driven through inspiration, and on an experience level they aimed to provide a different way to fly from what was currently on offer. Over time Virgin Atlantic continued to innovate with flight amenities most of us now take for granted including wi-fi on planes, charging stations under seats and flat beds. By anyone's stretch of the imagination, these things are not going to set the world alight. However, they certainly are rea-sons why the airline regularly features high on global industry award lists and is often cited as 'innovative' by the general population.[12]

Over the coming pages we will review the evolution of business and uncover why the old rules of business need to be broken. We will examine outliers – making the case that these rebels are no longer outsiders, but trailblazers of what leadership requires in the future of work. As much of our world has been overturned by technology we now take for granted, we will discover how the beginnings of Silicon Valley and its friction of doing well and doing good have laid the unstable foundation of what defines success. We are in a hotbed of change. We see this in the values people share around the world as well as in our future leadership. It is redefining the next C-suite, which has been accelerated as people work through the global impact of 2020.

The subject of leadership is a murky one these days. Historically it was easy. Leaders were self-defined, projected across news features and included people in positions of power such as the President of the United States. But much like the shift from bought to earned media, leaders as we are coming to know them are no longer placed on propped and purchased pedestals. Instead they are emerging organically, visibly identified by the real following and direct influence they have on others. It is murky because a leader is no longer a leader because they say so; a leader is now created by the people.

This book is as much about what qualities people identify with as it is about how to amass and emulate them. It is about how to become a true leader in today's radically changing business landscape, not necessarily defined by your role within a company or self-published books stating as much. You are a leader not because you say so, but because *they* say so.

So, what are people looking for? Where do people turn for leadership now? How is a leader defined if no longer self-defined? These are questions we will uncover and unpick throughout the book, looking at how every single person can start executing leadership traits that resonate in today's business landscape. This book argues that the democratization of leadership is now accessible to everyone looking to create real and impactful change in the world. This first requires understanding today's world better in the context of what has happened before. I will then outline a framework for you to tap into your own strength as a leader. By redefining leadership, we can pave the way for the future and recognize emerging patterns that will define your success and achievement.

A rebellious leader is within us all

As a child I was never one to break the rules. Instead I spent much of my time trying to fit in. Being mixed race Chinese–Canadian from divorced parents in a small suburb in Canada, my clothing choices were led by what the popular girls in my school wore. At no point in my formative years do I recall thinking independently or differently from anyone else, and nor did I want to. I was perfectly happy reading *The Babysitter Club* books in my bedroom and wishing my parents would buy me a pony.

As I grew up, this trend continued. I never had big ambitions to become an entrepreneur. In fact, when asked by my first-grade teacher whom I would want to work for I told her my aspiration was to be employed at the nearby Dairy Queen – a fast-food joint that specialized in soft-serve ice cream. I was not aiming high.

I spent much of my university years going through the motions and taking on whatever jobs were easy at the time. The inspiration to be my own boss was limited. The only person I knew that owned their own business was my dentist and I certainly did not want to spend a lifetime with my hands in someone else's mouth. So to say that waking up at 30 years old with countless entrepreneur awards under my belt and the sale of my first business for millions was a surprise would be a colossal understatement.

My journey has surprised even me. It is with this lens that I have constantly analysed my own launch as a rebel leader and over the years I noticed a pattern emerge. It turns out that my lack of knowledge and base-level naivety in business have allowed me to work in unrestricted ways. My lack of experience managing people has given me an opportunity to lead in a way that works for me, driven by my purpose. My lack of network in Britain where I launched my first business forced me to rely on making business decisions based on instincts rather than sage advice from mentors. In truth, I believe that my bold approach along with my lack of experience are what have made me successful.

The world today is a vastly different place than it was before the internet, which was not that long ago. It may surprise you that the internet only became publicly available in 1991, Google in 1998, and Facebook launched in a university dorm room in 2004. We now take these things for granted. They have become ubiquitous in our way of life, influencing personal ideologies, democracy and the world's value system. With so much change, it should therefore come as no surprise that we need to redefine our world – and the rules that go along with it.

The day-to-day workings of my first business

Upon accepting the role my first employee, Mark, got straight to work. The first stop was showing him where he was going to work and so we trekked the hundred yards down the narrow corridors into my shoe-box of an office. Not only was the description apt because of its size, which could only fit two desks side by side, it was also the storage room of a wedding shoe designer. With extraordinarily little revenue and zero savings, I was fortunate to have even found the space. It was the only office set-up that fit my budget and so I put up with working alongside walls of pale pink shoe boxes and stylist intrusions looking for the right size. If Mark was concerned about the office or the fact he had to work among high heels, he did not show it.

Despite our closet of an office, we worked well together. With computers side by side I was prone to micromanaging the tiniest of details I could see from his laptop. This drove him crazy. I had developed my attention to detail in a previous role in Canada raising funds for hospitals through home lotteries. These lotteries allowed people to pay substantially more for a ticket ($100) but had a very real chance of winning a home, boat or car. The funds (less the agency's commission) went to the hospital at the end of each lottery.

As the new girl on the team I was mostly given menial tasks such as photocopying and faxing, but the one time I was given a proofing job for a brochure I sent it to print with countless spelling mistakes. Granted, no one had explained proofing at the time, but that one mistake has carried me throughout my career. I learned the hard way that attention to detail was not just something someone had, it was something you had to build. Mark was very much like me, a big picture thinker. So, me constantly scrutinizing font size changes was likely not his ideal working scenario, but he persisted and never complained.

Over time Mark grew into the role, and the agency grew enough that we could move to a bigger office. We hired more staff and Mark became our most senior employee. Although it took nine months to secure my first full-time client, after proving my model was successful, it was not long before we started winning clients, including the artist formerly known as Prince and global brands such as Red Bull.

At no point did I ever think we were doing a great job – I always felt things could be done better. We could have always secured more or done more. I felt my job was never over and in that sense our agency culture became relentless in our efforts to do the best job every second of every day. This type of commitment became evident in everything we did and over time I started getting recognized for the work we did – winning industry accolades including the coveted *Media Week*'s 30 Under 30 award in 2012, a mere two years after launching my business.

In 2014, four years after launching, we were finally making enough money that I no longer felt the strain of paying rent or the panic of monthly salaries. I still was not making close to enough money to afford a down payment on an apartment in Central London, but with enough clients I could focus on the business's growth. I continued to run my agency by investing every penny we made back into the business to hire staff and keep those staff happy. Although we tended to pay less than our competitors in basic salaries, we heavily invested in training and experience – ensuring that even new graduate hires had the opportunity to travel abroad and sit in on senior sales meetings. I also ensured that we created opportunities for both individuals and teams – I would be the first to write an awards entry for an aspiring team member and the beer fridge was always stocked on Friday to celebrate the week's achievements.

Attending and entering industry awards was something I did every chance I had, a marketing tactic learned from my early days working on the Direct Marketing Association Awards, the flagship event at my last corporate job. I knew early on that most industry award shows were held for public relations purposes. This is not to say they are fixed, but that typically awards are won by those who put themselves forward for them, rather than by people and organizations chosen by independent jurors. Even if you do not win, it becomes a night to network among your peers and hopefully sweep up new clients along the way. If you do happen to win, then it becomes a great selling hook for new business.

One of the most notable award events in the United Kingdom, the Great British Entrepreneur Awards, was a highlight for me as it was known for recognizing the country's most enterprising minds. Prior to my attendance at the awards in 2014 I had been keeping my head down working tirelessly at the agency. Although I had entered a category, with fierce competition I did not expect I would be carrying any trophies home. It was on that cold winter's evening when I felt things started to change. Looking back, it became a pivotal point where I became aware that the industry I was working in was finally recognizing what we were doing. And not just the work and partnerships we built, but the fact that *we did things differently.*

Although I lost in my entered category, a surprise announcement was made that there were newly developed categories from the esteemed judges and I was jolted into action as a spotlight shone on our table and my name was called out. I had won the award for Media Disruptor of the Year.

It was not until my morning walk into the office with my buttery croissant in hand that I had a chance to reflect on what had happened. Rather than winning in a category that was reduced in numbers due to age (the Young Entrepreneur of the Year Award was given to entrepreneurs under 30 years of age), I had won an actual award that represented the entire industry. What was more, they had created this new award just for me. What they saw in what we were doing was that we were not afraid of breaking the rules. I became known as a rebel.

This small trophy, which sits on my shelf today, has become a reminder that leaders are not always created because they want to lead, but rather because they have a vision. In a time where passion and inspiration can truly change the world, never has a vision been more important.

But what about you?

I believe that anything is possible. I also believe that if I can do it, so can anyone else. I did not grow up dreaming of becoming a rebel leader. In truth, I am still flattered when anyone asks my business opinion or is interested in my way of doing things. It is this lack of self-belief that has allowed me to reflect on my path and find similar patterns in other leading entrepreneurs. It is my curiosity in understanding our current environment that has enabled me to develop a framework for a new type of leadership that is vastly different from what has come previously. In the coming pages, I hope to not only share my discovery, but also inspire a future generation to make change happen.

Disruption in the context of innovation is not a new term. Much has been written about these unique characteristics and how we might come to tap into them for success. In 2018 social entrepreneur Sam Conniff Allende drew comparisons between Golden Age pirates and challenging the status quo. His aptly titled book *Be More Pirate or How to Take on the World and Win* challenges our thinking to look at pirates as positive role models for change.[13] In his chapter 'Pirates vs Civilization Match Report' Allende outlines how fair pay, non-hierarchical structures, voting rights for women, on-the-job injury payouts, and the creation of cocktails – all launched by pirates – were hundreds of years ahead of their time. It seems we should have paid more attention to these rebel pirates then.

The slight challenge comes when trying to identify oneself as a pirate. It can be an extraordinary stretch for many. Furthermore, we often associate pirates with negativity, which makes it that much more challenging for us to then tap into their piratical characteristics. Perhaps if we recognized the achievements of these rebels as achievements and not radical one-offs, we might be further along. Perhaps if we saw a bit of ourselves in these pirates, we would not be so quick to dismiss their ways. The problem therein lies not with the actions of those rebels that have gone before, but with our inability to translate their methods into our everyday lives. Rebelliousness and leadership present similar challenges whereby the achievements of such labels seem too great for any one individual; therefore, they are quickly dismissed.

But that is changing.

We now have the ability to witness leadership inspiration beyond our boardrooms, enabling us to pick and choose leadership qualities and characteristics across multiple people, rather than having them embodied in one individual. We can witness activism and bravery beyond our own streets and participate in real-time mass movements that are happening thousands of miles away. Because of this, millions of rebel leaders are popping up everywhere, we are just not used to recognizing them or indeed naming them as leaders. However, in the following pages we will come to celebrate these rebellious traits and ultimately identify how you can replicate them.

You do not need to wait for that big promotion or until you have 50 staff to manage. New leadership starts with just one person. All you need is a framework to identify your purpose and a bit of rebelliousness to execute it. The rest, as they say, will follow.

This book encourages you to break all the rules and take an ideological leap of faith on radical potential. In yourself, in the world, in the future. We are now in an era where everything is possible and our ability to tap into that is no longer reserved for the elite. By understanding this new framework in the future of work, you will be able to lead its future with more possibility than ever before.

This is an exciting time for us all.

CHAPTER TWO

I built it in my bedroom

Necker Island, tech start-ups and the long journey back

I vividly remember my long dark hair flapping haphazardly in the wind. The boat was fast. Far faster than any boat I had been on before. On board with me were 18 tech entrepreneurs. The mood? You could cut the anticipation with a knife. Groups huddled together under the small safety of the boat's windshield against the Caribbean breeze, excitedly talking about what we'd find when we arrived at our destination.

Beside me, dressed in orange board shorts, brown flip-flops and a palm tree button-up, was Los Angeles-based Joe. As he spoke with his colleague, I eavesdropped on their conversation about seeing the zoo of endangered animals on the island. Apparently, there were more than 140 species including critically endangered lemurs and tortoises. Although impressed, as I had not heard this before, I was surprised this was the focus of their conversation. After all they were about to walk in to pitch to Sir Richard Branson on Necker Island in a bid to hopefully inspire the group of investors to part with up to $10 million.

One year earlier I decided to stop taking the lead on new clients as it was becoming overwhelming. As our client roster gained in both status and numbers, my sleep hours declined steadily. Although I had built up the agency to four global offices and notable clients including brands such as Shell and Hyundai, I was still investing every penny into its growth. Rather than spending money on senior staff on a higher pay grade, I made sure I filled the gaps and picked up any shortfall myself. Whether that was ordering the coffee or pitching a multi-million-dollar sponsorship proposal, I was always available and always on hand. But over five years of working every hour of every day with very little take-home salary myself, I started trying to pull back and regain some sanity.

However, it is very hard to say 'no' when new clients keep getting better. And the Extreme Tech Challenge was one of the best. Hosted on Necker Island with Sir Richard Branson, this was one of the world's largest start-up competitions for entrepreneurs addressing global challenges. These people were going to change the world and they wanted us to help them do it by securing new sponsors to grow their event. I was thrilled to be a part of it.

Among the thousands of entrepreneurs who entered, only the top 10 global finalists were invited to pitch on Necker Island. The prize: a chance to connect their innovations with a network of venture capital firms and investors who could provide significant funding to the top contenders. Ambitious in outcome and driven by a team of incredibly smart people, in my line of work it did not get much better.

We were serendipitously recommended as the agency to sell the event's sponsorship by a tech executive in Silicon Valley I had spoken to a year earlier. It was a mere three months after signing them as a client that I found myself on that speedboat jetting across the crystal blue waters of the British Virgin Islands to manage the sponsors onsite and understand how the event ran. My attendance was to learn as much about the event as possible in order for my agency to secure the millions in sponsorship required for the following year.

Although the time to sign up this fantastic new client was short, the travel time to arrive at the destination certainly was not. First, I took a nine-hour flight from London to Punta Cana, then I was shuffled onto a smaller plane to Beef Island. Upon arrival at Beef Island I grabbed my suitcase and trekked to the ferry boat packed with service industry professionals to cross to the small island of Virgin Gorda, the nearest island to Necker. Arriving in the evening after the hour-long ferry ride, I hauled my luggage through the unpaved parking lot lit by a single lamp to my pre-booked taxi, the back of a 1985 rusty red Chevy pickup truck that would take me an hour north where I would finally lay my head.

The following morning, cappuccino in hand, I was picked up on the dock of my hotel to catch a ride to Necker Island along with the hopefuls who were about to pitch their business to one of the greatest entrepreneurs of our time, Sir Richard Branson.

Getting to know the event inside and out, I spent the entire day speaking to the illustrious judging panel and excited applicants to discover what might benefit a potential sponsor. During my fact-finding mission, I was also encouraged to explore the island in order to start planning where events might be held the following year. Having worked backstage at many world-famous music festivals throughout my career, I did not think Necker Island would live up to the hype. How wrong I was.

Necker is just one of 60 islands that make up the British Virgin Islands, known for being the most exclusive and least developed of the Caribbean, which only adds to their appeal. Surrounded by clear turquoise waters with temperatures that rarely waver from a steady 28 degrees Celsius throughout the year, it is impossible not to instantaneously melt into the easy-going Caribbean culture, piña colada in hand. Of those

60 islands, Necker Island is the jewel in the crown and credited as one of Sir Richard Branson's 'best financial moves'.[1]

Despite the unaccustomed opulence that surrounded me on the 74-acre private island, it remains to this day one of the most tranquil places I have ever had the pleasure of visiting. Whether it's the exceptionally long transport time that provides enough of a buffer to truly sink into a relaxing state or the many staff who cater to your every possible need, you truly feel at home. This juxtaposition was not lost on me considering my actual home at the time was a cramped rented flat in London.

It was that afternoon that I took my first Instagram selfie standing barefoot on the sandy beaches of that island. I wanted to capture the memory. Etched in my brain as a work achievement of which by my own standards I had very few. I was just six years on from barely being able to afford rent and working in pyjamas in my freezing bedroom to being on one of the most famous private islands in the world. And I was getting paid to do it.

For those following my career on social media, I looked like an overnight success. I had quite literally gone from bedroom to boardroom in a few short years, sipping champagne with the world's top 1 per cent and providing commercial advice to tech start-ups that were shaping our future.

On social media everything looks easy. And glamorous. The truth behind the filters is that I worked exceptionally hard, but more importantly, capitalized on the change in business structure that was driven through the advance of technology and access to the internet. My business was agile. Its flat structure enabled me to move more quickly than my competitors and I invested heavily in areas where I saw even a sliver of potential for marginal growth. I charged through every open door (and some closed ones), followed up every lead and conversation. Against all advice given at the time, there was nothing I did not say 'yes!' to. If I was double-booked to speak at an event,

I coached my very junior (and very reluctant) team to get on stage. We never missed an opportunity. Ever.

Working at that pace is not for everyone. But if you want to go beyond what you think is possible, I do believe it is mandatory. Sacrificing your time, your money, your future in those early days can be the difference between success and failure. The difference between profitability and achievement. The realities of high-growth success are far less glitzy than popular media would suggest. It is the ability to push the boundaries in every area you are working towards just that little bit further.

As we explored in the first chapter with Dave Brailsford and his achievements with marginal gains and the British cycling team, small wins add up to greatness. It is not just about doing one big thing well; it is the culmination of doing many small things well that creates excellence. The more marginal gains you can achieve in every area of your business, the greater your chance of success.

However, in order to multi-task in such a way you must be able to put everything on the line and go all in. As Elon Musk is famously quoted as saying, 'My proceeds from the PayPal acquisition were $180 million. I put $100 million in SpaceX, $70 million in Tesla and $10 million in Solar City. I had to borrow money for rent.'[2]

I was thinking about that quote as the day on Necker Island turned into evening and we settled into our white wooden chairs surrounding the tennis court to listen to the pitches. There was a palpable buzz among the hundred-person audience made up of investors, sponsors and tech entrepreneurs, matched only by the rustling of the palm leaves blowing in the gentle breeze that surrounded us.

The pitches were polished, clearly rehearsed for days. Even the applicants' nerves could not be detected underneath their pressed white linen shirts. Once all pitches had been completed, the judges, led by Sir Richard Branson, scurried into the judging area. It was not created with secrecy in mind; instead plush sofas sat among the wooden indoor-outdoor living space located above the bar where the attendees sat waiting for the verdict. So as not to give away any hints to potential eavesdroppers below, these tycoons of industry sat elbow to elbow discussing which business model had the most potential. Although speaking very little during the actual debate, it was clear Sir Richard Branson's small but noteworthy interjection at the end made the final decision.

The trophy was awarded to Vantage Robotics, a compact aerial camera drone manufacturer that won based on the potential it had in the market compared with the other start-ups. Once the trophy was handed off, the party began. As a group we trekked 15 minutes up the hill to the main residence where a gourmet dinner awaited. Without a seating plan, everyone strategically crowded the main table waiting until Sir Richard Branson took his seat. Chaos quickly ensued with 20 vying young hopefuls trying to get any seat within earshot of the island's legendary owner. I had the pleasure of sitting next to our DJ for the evening, Mix Master Mike – famous for his work with the Beastie Boys. Having spent the morning, afternoon and much of the early evening in deep conversation about artificial intelligence and the future of robotics, it was refreshing to talk about whether Mike or I would make it to the rumoured 5 am last call and wishing we were still 20 years of age.

After a night spent dancing on the beach under the stars, I haphazardly made it back to my hotel room where I caught the faint glimpses of dawn as I fell asleep with my shoes on.

The democratization of big business

I spoke to nine tech start-up companies during my time on Necker Island. Although their businesses varied greatly from an easy-application haemorrhage gel that stopped bleeding to technology-driven personalized prenatal healthcare, the common theme was that all these businesses were relatively light in terms of physical company assets. Most had gone through a Series A round of funding, raising between $2 million and $15 million through angel investors or venture capital, but were structured incredibly thin with minimal overheads. I also noticed that while all CEOs were connected to their companies via their phones, none seemed too concerned with being out of the office.

As the Extreme Tech Challenge annually reviews the future of business and specifically awards those that will affect change in our world, this small, unique sample is indicative of what lies ahead. Despite the glamour of the competition's location, the fact that these business structures – regardless of which country they originated from – were all similar in nature is hugely telling. A reflection of a wider shift that is occurring globally. This lean and nimble structure contrasts the big legacy corporate businesses that used to rule venture capital funding. And it is this shift away from physical assets which has significant implications for what new traits are required for future leaders.

As recently as 1996 when penny stock Bre-X Minerals soared to a valuation of over CAD $6 billion, the story memorialized by Matthew McConaughey in the movie *Gold*, the perceived value of tangibility from business assets you could touch and see was high. When it was discovered that the gold mine was in fact a scam, the shockwave was felt globally. Millions of people lost billions of dollars. It impacted everyone.

With the story of loss splashed on the news, our love of gold and our emotional security in tangible assets dropped considerably. This not only affected investors but became a news story that affected everyone's ideals around investment security. It proved that despite infrastructure, funding and Wall Street predictions, your retirement plan could all come crashing down in an instant. The fear that something that seemed so tangible

– as nothing is more tangible than gold – could be a complete fabrication was a wakeup call to take businesses that may have fewer tangible assets on the balance sheet more seriously.

Small steps of investment in these areas have paid off, many becoming the tech unicorns of our time. The advancement of technology alongside the value of building a brand has replaced the overreliance on gold. Unlike gold, these tech unicorns can exponentially drive share prices in record time to deliver shareholder value. This tech investment bubble has driven the value of intangible assets exponentially, proving to the world that businesses are now able to build profit without bricks and mortar. Historically unheard of.

Augmenting this sentiment is the unprecedented ability for businesses to directly access customers for zero cost. This ability to benefit from being a global brand without the historic costs incurred is unprecedented, creating not just access to new customers anywhere in the world but the ability to gain global insight and information to support businesses' growth and decision making. In 2018 alone e-commerce represented 40 per cent of the sales growth in the consumer-packaged goods sector in the United States.[3] Considering that the first online transaction was made in 1994, the growth of this completely new distribution channel is a unicorn unto itself in terms of business functioning and growth.[4]

Although technology launched this new business structure, it has been the antiquated and traditional sectors that have been quicker to integrate and disrupt historical models. When old rules of legacy prevent growth and change for substantial periods of time, unrest builds. One of the first sectors to undergo this profound shift was the beauty industry.

Beauty now knows no bounds

Despite its obsession with promoting the very latest in trends, the beauty industry has been monopolized for the last 50 years by just 10 companies which controlled 70 per cent of the make-up market. Beauty monopolies were built on heritage (L'Oréal launched in 1909) and drove products to consumers through experience and nostalgia. With most revenue rung up at the beauty counter in your local department store, it was these long-standing retail relationships between beauty brand and shop owner that made entering the $532 billion industry impossible without exceptionally deep pockets.[5] The growth in net profits of these global beauty brands – often seeing an annual growth of 17 per cent – was driven through availability on shelves and a growing ageing population, rather than beauty trends or under-standing actual consumer needs. Arguably a legacy beauty brand's business strategy was to ignore much of the population, instead focussing on one segment – white middle-aged women.

Although this may seem discriminatory, it unfortunately also made business sense. In the fast-moving consumer goods envi-ronment, consumer preferences are the quickest way to eat into profits. In any manufacturing plant, the highest rate of pro-duction will be one product as there is only one set-up required. As you increase the number of products made in any given plant, the amount of production decreases due to the time it takes to change the supply line over. By streamlining product offerings, beauty brands could ensure higher profitability against their significantly large cost of manufacturing. This was then compounded by being able to purchase larger quantities of both ingredients and marketing material to capitalize on economies of scale.

This narrowed focus on one type of beauty was widely accepted until music artist Rihanna's Fenty Beauty burst on the scene (created in partnership with French luxury goods conglom-erate LVMH). Fenty Beauty made headlines by launching 40 foundation shades – the darkest of which sold out first – in September 2017. Despite leading the beauty industry for the past century with a minimal offering, L'Oréal quickly followed suit a few months later, increasing their original 23 shades of

True Match Foundation to the new industry standard set by Rihanna of 40 shades.

Fenty Beauty did not just make waves by offering more foundation shades for more women, they cleverly harnessed the low-cost marketing opportunity presented by social media to promote their vision to the masses. It was clearly what the people wanted and within just 15 months of launching, Fenty Beauty generated an estimated $570 million in revenue.[6] While this seems like an enormous amount for what was effectively a start-up business, by comparison it was only 2 per cent of what L'Oréal took in the same period.[7] What is impressive here is not necessarily the revenue secured, but the fact that Fenty Beauty managed to generate an entirely new market by bypassing the clientele L'Oréal had solely focussed on for over a century. And Rihanna is not the only one leading from the front.

In an episode of the reality TV show *Keeping Up with the Kardashians* titled 'Lip Service' which aired on 10 May 2015, youngest Kardashian Kylie Jenner's plumped-up lips drove the storyline. The episode featured family arguments between Kylie and her siblings (particulary Kim Kardashian), who were upset about lying to the public as Kylie continued to tell the media that her drastically changed lip shape was created by make-up and not plastic surgery. At just 17 years of age, being in the public eye is understandably a lot of pressure to handle during a time of developing confidence.

But this 17-year-old might have been playing the public all along, building the hype of her lips within a show that she starred in. A year before the 'Lip Service' episode aired, she signed a contract with Seed Beauty, the company that manufactures her now famous Kylie Cosmetics beauty products. Founded by siblings Laura and John Nelson in 2014, Seed Beauty is a beauty brand incubator that takes the partnership model to a new level. Unlike traditional legacy brands like L'Oréal, Seed Beauty is known by beauty experts as 'an entrepreneurial brand lab. Its whole reason for being is not to follow any industry rules'.[8] It is through this rebellious stance that it has become one of the leading beauty companies, although almost unknown to any consumer. Seed Beauty brings the fast-fashion model to the beauty industry. But rather than taking the runway to the high street as fast-fashion leader Zara does, Seed Beauty underpins its decisions and collaborations from social media. What is most remarkable is its ability to take a product from conception to creation in just five days, compared with L'Oréal which averages two years. Seed Beauty is arguably on a different playing field, leading a gap in the market that will only continue to widen.

Kylie Cosmetics started just like the other tech entrepreneurs I met on Necker Island did – agile. In fact, the first 15,000 Kylie lip kits were funded by Jenner at a cost of just $250,000[9] and involved only six employees. Five years later with a valuation of $1.2 billion,[10] you might be surprised to learn that growth in revenue does not necessarily demand a growth in physical assets. In line with the original business structure, Jenner keeps the business exceptionally light and currently manages with just 12 employees. Understanding that value in a business goes beyond tangible assets, Jenner has sweated every angle to amass her beauty fortune, much to the shock of the legacy brands that monopolized the market for over a century.

What makes Kylie Cosmetics an indication of a new business model in the future of work? It is not her celebrated ability to take a selfie, but rather her desire to do something authentic and break the rules that were put in place before her. In more than one hundred years many independent beauty brands have tried, and failed, to take market share. Beauty brands that had connections, had vision, even had their own followings and brand ambassadors – but none were successful, until now.

And why is that? Why has it only now been possible to be successful through disruption in the past decade? As we will come to explore in the following pages, it is because we finally have both the tools and the access to democratize big business.

This ability to democratize is being driven by two main factors: social media and direct-to-consumer.

Social media and authenticity

Social media has provided an opportunity for anyone, anytime, anywhere to share. Our strong desire to communicate has fuelled a never-ending fire of information, and we still want more. It is this relentless flow of new information that is critical to understanding the shift in our decision-making process. Important because the onslaught of information received is reshaping our brains by changing our neuronal structures, allowing us to absorb more information at a quicker pace over time. We already see this in the brains of illiterate people, which are structurally different from those of people who can read.[11]

But if we are altering our brains to create new decision pathways, it begs the question: can we trust the information that we receive?

Our new normal is about transparency and authenticity, or at least the perception of both. Although we still love to watch a polished television advertisement, we no longer believe in them. In fact, just a paltry 4 per cent of consumers trust ads.[12] Instead the overwhelming majority of people (74 per cent) make their buying decisions based on social media.[13] People are much more media savvy, more likely to trust information that is received in real time with less editing and manipulation.

By pulling away the smokescreen of polished advertisements, social media empowers consumers to make better decisions. It also provides more choice, enabling the individual to highly curate their world around their own specific set of ideologies. We now can feel more original, propelling our desire to choose products that define us. This is vastly different from the historical push of products where choice was limited and what was right for you was crafted in the glossy papers of your favourite magazine.

But this shift away from advertisements to social media in order to create a more authentic self is not one-sided. Instead it is on a constant feedback loop as people upload their choices, effectively their ideology, onto social media. What becomes interesting is when those individuals who may feel outside of the majority in their offline world find that they are not as alone online as they might have once thought. It is this connection that allows people to feel safer in their own skin than previously possible and it is revealing this difference on a mass scale which has grown online networks beyond what we could have imagined possible just 20 years ago.

Confidence and self-worth are then derived from our sense of purpose. We now have our own tribe. But being part of an online collective is not a passive activity. Instead there is an intrinsic instinct to provide value in the form of useful and valuable information to our tribe. This is the opposite of an advertisement. Thus, the feedback loop continues propelled by authenticity which should provide trust in ensuring that the recommendation made is the *right* recommendation.

It is this authenticity that has seen Jenner's fortune skyrocket. Initially credited by *Forbes* as the youngest female billionaire in 2019 (later retracted by the magazine which now estimates her net worth to be just under $900 million), the fact she made $590 million in 2019 from selling the majority of Kylie Cosmetics is no mean feat for a 21-year-old.[14] Comparing that to Facebook founder Mark Zuckerberg who hit billionaire status at the age of 23, it is a substantial achievement. Especially considering the fortune was amassed through an infamous pout and some lip kits. With over 110 million followers on social media a cynic might assume Jenner's product choice was solely designed to target her following of young women. But when you uncover that Jenner's insecurities are what drove her to create something to boost her own self-confidence, you can identify a very real difference in how Kylie Cosmetics executes compared with traditional brands, more likely to start product development with a focus group rather than a celebrity self-esteem issue. Jenner herself describes her decision to use her former insecurity and turn it into a positive as 'one of the most authentic things I've done in my career.'[15]

The beauty industry has come a long way from the days of door-to-door selling and neighbourhood block beauty parties of Avon.

Direct-to-consumer: access anytime, anywhere

Authenticity and adding value would be useless unless the audience in question could act on that information, which is why direct-to-consumer e-commerce is quickly becoming the world's most important retail channel. Supported by accessibility where the tap of a button can transact up to $40 million for a single e-commerce purchase, even in the remotest of towns you can still access the latest trends.

Direct-to-consumer speeds up the ability to get a product to market by utilizing the relationship built between a product and its customer. No longer requiring heavy upfront investment in infrastructure, focus groups and advertising campaigns, brands gain immediate feedback through social media – a win–win for both the consumer and the product teams themselves. This has sped up the process of creation and advancement, putting consumers at the heart of business.

Frustratingly, this power shift has not been easily incorporated by legacy brands, many of which have launched social media campaigns out of necessity, the whitewash of which has not gone unnoticed by consumers. Their lack of authenticity is why most of these social media campaigns fail.

As online consumers we are now actively part of this consumer-brand dynamic regardless of how or what we buy. We now have power. This is a significant shift away from the concept of traditional advertising and lays the foundation for new rules in the future of work.

It goes beyond influencer marketing

You would be forgiven for assuming that fast trends and a sea of online followers are the only two pieces necessary to unlock success in this radically changing low-cost, high-growth business environment. In fact, the concept of influencer marketing that helps turn 'likes' into cash is sought after by most. Who wouldn't want to earn a living by posting content on social media? It has become such big business that the industry is projected to reach up to $15 billion by 2022, despite Facebook only being available to users around the world since 2016 and TikTok just one year later.[16]

Influential *Forbes* magazine has even got in on the action by publishing ratings for the top influencers' ability to drive brand value.[17] And with FTSE 100 companies falling over themselves trying to work with these online super-sellers, social media has become the belle of this new ball. With up to 100,000 followers, any Instagram blogger could earn up to $5,000 for one post. Considering there are over 1 billion users on Instagram alone, influence can be big business for anyone with access to a smartphone.[18] But true influence is not as easy as social media suggests and even some of the world's largest brands have made that mistake.

No stranger to utilizing celebrities and animated characters to push products, Disney was one of the first to jump on the social media influencer bandwagon to gain a competitive edge. In an effort to stay relevant, Disney purchased Maker Studios, a YouTube network of online creators and influencers, for an initial $500 million in 2014. The purchase included a further payout of $450 million if aggressive growth targets were met. But as fake bots became pervasive and influencers shifted the focus of valuable content to pushing #ads, so too did the power of the actual influence. Disney felt this more than most and after a final payout of just $675 million for Maker Studios it became clear that millions of followers did not always equate to bottom line sales.

Upon reflection a former Maker Studios executive stated:

Disney saw the MCN gold rush, went prospecting and said, 'We're going to buy the biggest, shiniest one. If this becomes something, it's worth having the biggest.' I don't think they knew what they were buying. And quite honestly, I don't think there was much to buy.[19]

So, if one of the biggest brands in the world can make an oversight in thinking any influencer with a following can drive leadership, you can be forgiven. Like Disney, it is easy to assume that the only success stories in this new radical business framework are the ones splashed out on *Forbes* or *GQ*. However, real influence is established through authenticity. Real authenticity does not require millions of followers. Instead its utilization can be executed in the smallest of ways. It is the impact that is now becoming immeasurable and can be replicated if guided by simple principles.

Small following, big influence

One frosty morning on 29 January 2019 a cascade of bundled-up leggy models, discerning press and global trendsetters descended on the hygge capital of the world for Copenhagen Fashion Week in Denmark. What the global fashion event may lack in couture status from Paris and the FROW (front row) celebrities found in Milan, it makes up for in relevance. Putting a focus on wearable, tasteful fashion, it is often quoted as the show with the best street style. Core to capturing this street style, the media – fundamental to promoting the trends to the world – brace against the icy temperatures in droves.

Despite the 32 brands showing at the star-studded event throughout the week, the fashion label that made some of the biggest headlines globally was a brand that did not even have a runway show. In fact, the label in question had never had a runway show, ever. With limited budgets having only launched a year earlier in 2018, they could not afford to. Unbelievably, they were not even in attendance.

How is it possible for a fashion label that did not have a runway show, had absolutely no advertising or marketing presence during Copenhagen fashion week, and that did not even attend, manage to capture the pages of our coveted fashion magazines? To discover the answers, we must break the rules we think manage social media influence.

M.92 founding sisters Maryam and Amina Mamilova believe the significant press they gained at Copenhagen fashion week despite not being there was down to their intuition. They are the first to admit that they do not see themselves as savvy business-people or even as experienced designers (they have degrees in international journalism and classical studies). Their love of design comes from their grandmother who was a skilled seam-stress. Business decisions to date have been made on intuition. Despite launching without a clear plan of action or expectation, it seems their intuition has paid off – outperforming some of the savviest of independent fashion labels.

'We just try to figure things out on the go and jump at every opportunity to learn something new, which doesn't always come easy to us,' Maryam Mamilova told me. 'Getting a runway show or hiring a publicist definitely wasn't our preferred course of action. First because it is very costly, but second because it felt too commercialized which just wasn't us.'[20]

Unlike the Kylie Jenners of this world, M.92 have just a few thousand followers on their Instagram page. Their investment into their pieces is so focussed that they do not even have a website. Being digital natives, they chose to limit their expenses to the bare minimum and utilized all the free channels available to them, cleverly choosing to sell exclusively from their free Instagram account rather than pay for a Shopify or e-commerce website. All orders are taken through direct message with customers and payments transacted through PayPal. Much like the launch of their brand, the radical decision to exclusively use a free platform as their distribution channel was one that evolved through their engagement with their customers and not a planned strategic business move. Mamilova reflects:

> It's not that we don't want a website, it just so happened that in the process of creating one we realized that we enjoy connecting with our customers on a more personal level.
>
> The benefit of using Instagram is that there is no mediator, no retail mark-up, and you feel completely in control. This is essential for our desire to manufacture a narrative underpinned by a highly personalized meaning. There is nothing separating us from our audience. The benefit of using the platform also means we have access to all these amazing people who might like our product and buy it directly.

And buy it they did. It was at Copenhagen fashion week that freelance fashion stylist Emili Sindlev was snapped wearing one of M.92's signature cotton floral frocks, an image that was later posted to her 350,000 followers. Later that day other fashion influencers were spotted in similar dresses, one of the most notable being *ELLE UK* editor Daisy Murray.

The opposite of fast fashion, M.92 produce extremely limited quantities of their stock, but pride themselves on using some of the best fabrics on the European market and paying fair wages to everyone they work with. Their focus on craftsmanship and sustainability aligns exceptionally well with the goals of the week-long event that launched them into the forefront of fashion.

The fashion show itself is also evolving. Taking a radical stance to shift Copenhagen fashion week to become 'a platform for advocacy', chief executive Cecilie Thorsmark wants to use her event to make a real difference. Launching an ambitious sustainability action plan, participating brands now must meet 17 sustainability targets including bringing in zero-waste set designs, using at least 50 per cent organic or recycled textiles in their collections and pledging to not destroy unsold clothing. Bans for the week include single-use plastic bottles and plastic coat hangers.[21] These new rules are a direct attack on the waste and excess that previous fashion week organizers have championed. They are also indicative of new rules in the future of work.

Thorsmark is not merely making this push as a means to differentiate from her much larger fashion week competitors, but rather utilizing her event to spearhead the values of the host city, Copenhagen being one of the most environmentally friendly cities in the world with aims to become the world's first carbon neutral capital city by 2025. And it is this focus on values, rather than ad spend, that laid the foundations for M.92 to become one of the most talked-about brands of the week.

As this chapter has demonstrated, big business no longer requires cold hard cash to outstrip the competition. You do not need millions of followers to capitalize on the new future of work. The internet has made customers, marketing, distribution and access virtually free – the only thing left for a leader to do is put real thought and effort into their execution.

Big businesses like L'Oréal are being challenged by new leaders who think and act differently. These new leaders are not focussed on creating a market, but instead on creating products for existing markets that may have been overlooked in the past. This is a vastly different concept from what has been done previously, producing new successes. Successes that are no longer confined by old rules. Successes that know no boundaries. And in this radically new way of working, we require new types of leaders.

Out with the old, in with the new

The traits of successful leaders today are vastly different from those of the past. Historically leadership within big business was granted on self-proclamations and the characteristic of steering a big ship in one direction that pushed the business forward.

These leaders were often found climbing the corporate ladder and pushing their ideologies from a command and control tower.

As Rihanna, Kylie Jenner and M.92 have proven, it is listening rather than shouting that is winning the war in the future of work. Listening to the world, listening to the market, listening to what people *really* want and then having the courage to go out and make it happen. Because if you do not, you may not be around for much longer. Leaders who disregard these monumental shifts in the future of work are being left behind, as indicated by the CEO departures that have been steadily trending upwards since August 2018. In January 2020 CEO exits hit a monthly record of 172, which came after 2019 marked the biggest year ever with 1,600 exits.[22] This is clearly not a time for leaders to stick their heads in the sand.

Along with leaders, traditional businesses are also getting the shakedown. Social media has made customer advocacy transparent and means that legacy brands can no longer rely on history, complacency and strong ties to a few. Customers are enforcing the need for value and ethics through their involvement with brands online. Finally, it seems that the needs of the many now have a voice to outweigh the stalwarts of the few. Old businesses and old business models are quickly losing traction, giving rise to new leaders who understand the new rules in the future of work. This is not just about losing the high street; this is about giving people what they really want.

The power of the people in this new customer and business dynamic is hugely influential and has only been made possible by our access to the internet. But it is not just our credit cards and purchase power that have shifted; it is our shifting ideologies and values alongside them. The interconnectivity of how we engage with the world through our purchases and through our thoughts is a fundamental driver of this shift. But before we look to understand these new rules in this rapidly changing world, it is important to first contextualize the foundation from which it was all built – Silicon Valley.

And as with the Peter Parker principle, 'With great power comes great responsibility', so too are we realizing far too late that businesses that can change our world for the better can also change our world for the worse. In the following chapter we will explore how conflicting values in Silicon Valley laid an unsteady foundation and created the global discord that we are only now beginning to try to rectify.

CHAPTER THREE

'Move fast and break things' is broken

The foundations of the internet were laced with LSD

From the mid-1990s when first the internet and then the world wide web became accessible to the public, the excitement of a revolution and the feeling of an impending transformation for our time were palpable. It felt like the future was here.

As the previous two chapters illustrated, the internet created more potential and possibility than ever before – especially as it relates to business and leadership. If information is power, then we felt we finally had it. We could turn our dreams into realities. The whole world was quite literally at our fingertips. The positive impact of the internet was not just a new tool, it became a new global consciousness.

In a 1995 column for *Wired* magazine, Nicholas Negroponte, founder of MIT's Media Lab, wrote:

Being digital is positive. It can flatten organizations, globalize society, decentralize control, and help harmonize people... In fact, there is a parallel... between open and closed systems and open and closed societies. In the same way that proprietary systems were the downfall of once great companies like Data General, Wang and Prime, overly hierarchical and status-conscious societies will erode. The nation-state may go away. And the world benefits when people are able to compete with imagination rather than rank.[1]

Although Negroponte's prediction seemed to be materializing, the path to benefiting the world has been a rocky one. We had hoped our access to information would be enough for change to happen, yet there remains underlying unrest. A decade later people began taking the fight for an open society into their own hands as illustrated by the #MeToo movement and Black Lives Matter.

This proves that there is tension lying under the surface threatening to erupt as our hopes for a better world have yet to transpire. The world is frustrated. We see what is possible and we have the tools to make change happen, but change has yet to be fully realized. We are only just scratching the surface on the transformation that was promised in the 1990s. What is now required is the right leadership to progress. The right leadership to change the world into a better place for all.

This desire is not new. Most recently, the fight for change and freedom was memorialized by the hippie movement of the 1960s and 1970s. Rising in part as opposition to the US involvement in the Vietnam War, these communes promoted counterculture and to the untrained eye would be radically opposed to the technologies of dehumanization, centralized bureaucracy and the rationalization of social life. Ironically, it was this hippie culture that gave rise to the countercultural dream of empowered individualism and collaborative community that computers now promote just a few decades on.

The story of computers and how they have been utilized for the promotion of human ideologies is fascinating. But more than a good story is the understanding of how this determination of tool use for the greater good is currently at odds with the concept of doing well. This tension has built up in Silicon Valley and is seeping out into the rest of the world. The feelings of unrest are justified. They were put in place at the very beginning.

To understand how this came to be and why tension currently exists in our relationship with technology and our personal career motivations, we turn to San Francisco and the man who started it all, Stewart Brand.

Set in northern California alongside the ocean, San Francisco is a haven. Known for its cool summers, steep rolling hills, the Golden Gate Bridge, cable cars and Alcatraz, it is a tourist's dream. But beyond tourism, it is also known for being the centre of liberal activism in the United States. With its history steeped in the Gold Rush, an active port of embarkation for service members in World War II, and the birthplace of the United Nations, the location was a perfect hotbed for Americans to flock to and discuss key issues of the time.

In addition to the intellectuals, the city itself helped spark contemplation – namely its rooftops. The uneven skyline of San Francisco is beautiful from the rooftop, with a glimpse of the ocean on all three sides of the city. The rolling hills that make the trolley service so inviting create a vision of both static depth and movement as the sun rises and sets across the eclectic mix of multi-coloured Victorian homes. A view that is both breathtaking and inspirational. Exactly the type of setting required to inspire a movement.

Although starting a movement was not exactly on Stewart Brand's agenda as he climbed through his window to take to his apartment roof on a cold February in 1966, it comes as no surprise that this is where it all began. In a town of philosophers, he was a man known for getting things done – especially when he was inspired. Just one month prior he helped launch The Trips Festival – promoted as a transformative event that helped mark the beginning of the hippie counterculture movement in San Francisco. When the big idea was pitched to him the year before, Brand recalled, 'I knew in my heart they were not going to be able to pull that off, but that it ought to happen. So I picked up the phone.'[2] With Brand on board, the three-day event was attended by over 10,000 people and included performances by the Grateful Dead and Big Brother pre-Janis Joplin. It was a huge success.

On his rooftop, aided by 100 micrograms of lysergic acid diethylamide (LSD) and wrapped in a blanket to fight the bitter cold wind rushing off the Pacific Ocean, 28-year-old Brand collected his thoughts. He liked thinking in this way; it aligned with his counterculture drive against boredom and uncertainty. It was his one-person assault against the rigidity he grew up with that defined cold-war technocracy and allowed him to dream of a utopian future built around communes and communities.

As the LSD kicked in, the skyline shifted. The static buildings concaved, and the pressure of the world was felt underneath the gravity of change. This visual representation of the curvature of the Earth sparked a memory of a lecture Brand had heard from Buckminster Fuller, who was renowned for his comprehensive perspective on the world's problems, stating that the root of all misbehaviour stemmed from people perceiving the Earth as flat.[3] It seemed to Brand an obvious solution in that moment that the simple fix for a better world was to then show people that the world was round.

Scribbled into his journal that night was the question: 'Why haven't we seen a photograph of the entire Earth yet?'[4]

By then the space race between the Soviet Union and the United States was on. Acting as another dramatic arena for cold-war competition, the ability to showcase technology and claim superiority was owning the next frontier. The Sputnik launch in

1957 by the Soviets prompted the United States into action. NASA increased their budget by almost 500 per cent and President John F Kennedy made the bold and public claim that the United States would land a man on the moon before the end of the 1960s.[5]

While all this was going on it dawned on Brand that while much had been done in space, there existed no actual photograph in space looking back towards the Earth.

It was this single idea that launched his button campaign, pins used to convey political statements, onto the streets and universities of California asking the very same question: 'Why haven't we seen a photograph of the whole Earth?' Sending buttons to NASA and members of Congress, Brand would eventually get the first colour photograph of the whole Earth just a year later in 1967. This photograph became a symbol, a visual representation of doing good and being better. Unsurprisingly it was this photograph that Brand chose to mark one of his greatest achievements, the *Whole Earth Catalog*. Used on the front cover of the first edition, the whole Earth can be seen against a flat backdrop of heavy blackness with a simple subtitle 'access to tools'. It was this *Whole Earth Catalog*, a counterculture magazine and product catalogue published by Brand several times a year between 1968 and 1972, that many credit with having 'changed the world'.[6]

The premise 'access to tools' was a life guide for all people living on Earth, but its use tended to be reserved for communes who needed to upskill themselves when living off the grid. Information made living in this way possible. The notion that anyone in the world could find information on anything to help shape their lives and their environment was revolutionary at the time. The editions and pages knew no bounds. Information was provided in areas as diverse as organic farming, solar power, recycling, wind power, desktop publishing, mountain bikes, midwife-assisted birth, female masturbation, computers and goat husbandry. By the sheer level of its far-reaching diversity in topics, discussions around technology became eloquently woven into counterculture as a force for change. It laid the framework for an impactful mindset shift that computers could be helpful to humans. Computers could become tools for the people.

The *Whole Earth Catalog* is eloquently summarized by John Markoff, a technology writer for *The New York Times*, as 'the internet before the internet. It was the book of the future. It was a web in newsprint'.[7] It became a symbol of what were arguably the first seedlings of the world wide web. So influential this book has been in shaping Silicon Valley and the world we now live in that Steve Jobs credited the *Whole Earth Catalog* as 'one of the bibles of my generation'.[8]

If it seems far-fetched that a catalogue of information could change the world in the sixties it is because we have all grown so accustomed to our direct and immediate access to information as standard. But it was not until Brand made the direct connection between personal tools and computers that our thinking was transformed, away from the computer's initial military use to tools that can help everyone.

To Brand, computers made utopia seem possible.

Alas, we have yet to achieve what Brand ambitiously set out to do on that rooftop over half a century ago. The inertia that has existed since Pandora opened the box of free information has grown larger, driving anxiety among the most zen in California. This inertia has swelled into a realization that the internet has changed our world, but potentially not all for the better. Since 2016 with the shock results of both the US election and the United Kingdom's Brexit vote, people are rightfully questioning their privacy, data and democracy. In a post-truth world, the rules are blurred, and truth be told, not even the rule makers know who they are and what their role is.

In the coming pages we will review how this tension between doing good and doing well has radically shifted the values of our world and the people living within it. We will cover the basic ideology of the general population as well as specifics on work–life balance. We now have the tools Brand initially aimed to give us, but if leaders are to lead, it is mandatory to look at what ideals are sought so that we indeed go in the direction we desire.

If leading with purpose can change the world, what purpose should be vindicated? Knowing what we know now, what do we care about most and can we, like Brand, aim to synthesize two diametrically opposing views of doing good and doing well? We will explore this concept in the following pages and outline the uncertainty that the personal computer has exposed in our way of life. This exposure is felt by everyone and movements both big and small are radically shifting the way in which we live and work, ultimately transforming the way in which we must lead.

Computers for evil

The transformation of the faceless military computer into one that could be used to liberate us happened quickly. Its progression into our homes and our hearts has been so routine very few questioned the direction or its impact in the future of work. The hippie values that it originated from carried throughout the launch of Facebook and the iPhone, before Google went public and before the dot-com bubble. It continued happily until it completely fell off a cliff in 2016 when we all witnessed from the discomfort of our soft sofas the shocking results in both the US election and the Brexit vote and the rise of political extremes that followed.

In truth, very few predicted either outcome or could foresee a future where information would become harmful. We happily continued to blindly tap 'I agree' on our smartphones to upload Candy Crush for our commute, the latest in Hollywood gossip, and notifications on our university alumni. The reveal that years of deception masked as free information was like ripping an emotional bandage off – painful, surprising, and we are all dealing with the aftermath of scar tissue. From Brand's initial desire to provide information and tools to people in factually accurate ways, our inherent assumption is that the information we receive online is true. Even Wikipedia which collates information from multiple sources aims to present the truth by combining multiple accounts. The entire premise of free information accessible to all is that the information helps us make better decisions. Our ability to make better decisions would allow us to then navigate the world more easily – ideally helping us make progress and achieve success. Aside from internet trolls and cyberbullying, discussions on big business manipulating information to deceive entire populations were outrageous.

The bombshell that inaccuracies were not just commonplace online, but that lies were being actively used to corrupt our very freedom, our elections and our minds stunned the world. It created such a shock to our ideologies that it was all anyone could talk about. Unsurprisingly, Oxford Dictionaries announced that the Word of the Year for 2016 was 'post-truth'.[9] Post-truth being a catchall term used to explain the shocking outcomes of reality-TV star and real estate mogul Donald Trump becoming the leader of the free world and the United Kingdom deciding that smaller must be better, contrary to a history of war to amass territory.

Post-truth describes an environment in which people are less influenced by factual information than by their emotions or personal beliefs and options. The term has been in existence for the past decade, but its move from being a peripheral term to widely understood in the course of a year demonstrates the impact on everyone's consciousness. Twenty-eight books on the subject of post-truth have been published since the explosive year of 2016, but the true unmasking of this new reality was not generally understood until this story and its relevance became available on Netflix on 24 July 2019. Award-winning documentary

The Great Hack exposed the British data and political consulting firm Cambridge Analytica, reporting on how they allegedly manipulated entire populations through mis-appropriation of digital assets, data mining and data brokerage. Although the UK's Information Commissioner's Office found no evidence of political tampering to the extent the programme alludes to, the documentary did provide an eye-opening revelation on how misuse of data can be utilized to sway opinion.

We now know we exist in a world where information is corruptible, and in many cases just plain false. A world where the leaders we historically looked to for guidance and direction, and in part truth, are transparently obscuring the truth for their personal gain. Regardless of facts, the strategic communication of this information is driving change in thought as well as in action, and most often not for the better.

Using information to deceive

An early statement by Trump that was repeated multiple times throughout his first presidential campaign trail was that the murder rate in the United States was at a 45-year high. Unsurprisingly, there was a significant backlash from the press, but rather than retract his statement, he utilized it as an opportunity to further instil confusion by saying: 'The press never talks about it.' And it was true, the press did not talk about it because it was not factually accurate.[10] Not only was the statement factually incorrect, it transparently highlighted a campaign communications strategy that fostered a lack of safety in US communities, particularly the smaller towns where murder rates are not regularly tracked or reported on. Cleverly, Trump used one of our most basic motivations as identified in Maslow's hierarchy of needs to drive consideration of his vote. He tapped into the most primal of needs, the second in Maslow's hierarchy, safety – the first need being too difficult to target as our need for air, water, food, shelter, sleep, clothing and reproduction are things we can touch and see. Instead, Trump created insecurity among our need to feel safe, a motivation that is difficult to factualize as it is intangible. A need that one simple public statement could shake as we have no individual base measure for it.

But it is not just politics where deception is played out in the public forum. Volkswagen, known for its German engineering and often affectionately referred to as the 'people's car', was exposed in a deliberate emissions scandal in violation of the Clean Air Act, which passed in Congress in 1970. The Clean Air Act recognized the substantial pollution hazard of personal vehicles on the environment and was put in place to ensure that automotive manufacturers followed stringent standards to create healthier air. It is arguably the bare minimum that car manufacturers need to adhere to for the safety of our planet. But the people's car manufacturer had other plans. In a deliberate attempt to defraud the testing of their diesel cars, with which the company owned 70 per cent of the US market, Volkswagen intentionally installed software that would change the parameters of emissions set in a testing situation to meet the Clean Air Act standards. However, in a real-world driving situation, the parameters would reset and the nitrogen oxide emissions expelled were up to 40 times above what was acceptable. Volkswagen admitted to rigging 11 million of its diesel cars in this way.[11]

What is more telling in the context of acceptable truths is that Volkswagen spent years on a 'Clean Diesel' advertising campaign, the most popular ad being three older women arguing about whether or not diesel engines are indeed dirty. The ad campaign was aptly titled *Old Wives Tales*. To discover that clean diesel does not actually exist unveiled the extent of deception in advertising. US Department of Justice Deputy Attorney General Sally Q Yates stated: 'By duping the regulators, Volkswagen turned nearly half a million American drivers into unwitting accomplices in an unprecedented assault on our atmosphere.'[12]

As we have outlined with both Volkswagen and former President Trump, the impact of how information and personal computers can be used to manipulate public opinion is now at the forefront of everything from privacy and data protection to upcoming elections.

We now know it exists, but what are we doing about it?

Fighting for truth

Since publishing his eye-opening and timely book *Post-Truth: The New War on Truth and How to Fight Back* on 11 May 2017, one of the UK's most respected political journalists, Matthew d'Ancona, believes that change is finally afoot.[13] He notes that since 2017 there have been many efforts to address the issue of post-truth and the fact that big technology companies are acknowledging there even *is* a problem proves progress in itself. Although we still have a long way to go. The challenge is that most governments still have not got to grips with the scale or even the nature of the phenomenon. D'Ancona states that to truly solve the issue of fake news and disinformation we require 'big thinking and big battles', which have yet to take place on a global stage.[14] Instead we are overwhelmed with the proliferation of conspiracy theories. These conspiracy theories help provide order to our existing chaos. And as our fear increases, so too does our desperation to grasp onto an explanation, any explanation, in certain circumstances. Often the greater the fear, the greater the conspiracy.

We saw this play out with Covid-19. As the pandemic raged, so too did conspiracy theories. Our daily online news feeds promoted theories that the virus was linked to 5G technology. Meanwhile, QAnon believers are circulating the 'mole children' theory, stating that the virus is a ploy to arrest members of the satanic 'deep state' whose alleged members include Tom Hanks, Barack Obama and Hillary Clinton, in order to release their sex-slave children hostages who are being held captive underneath

Central Park. Although these ranged from minor to the absurd, these theories should not be dismissed because they are moulding viewpoints during the greatest health risk this generation has ever seen.

With so much information available during a time when the world is reaching its tipping point, leadership becomes vital. But if accurate information is fundamental to provide guidance, how can one become a leader if their reality is skewed?

Fortunately, d'Ancona has the solution and remains ever the optimist when considering the future. Truth, he told me, is the antidote:

> My deepest conviction is that truth will survive and prosper as a core human ideal because no social order can really exist for very long without it. It is central to science, law, political accountability and real social justice. The problem is two-fold: first we have a technological revolution that appeases emotion instead of bolstering truth. That is what an algorithm does.
>
> Second: truth is *hard*. It is hard to confront the truth about a world as complex, nuanced and full of uncertainty as ours. It is easier to shout that Covid-19 is a 'Chinese virus' than it is to focus on the horrendously complicated business of preventing its spread and finding treatments and therapies. It is easier to deny climate science than it is to change absolutely the way we travel, eat, consume, invest.

In small and in big ways new leaders are emerging to fight this battle because truth is the foundation from which to build effective leadership. These fights are taking place publicly in the United States Congress, led by unlikely political leaders such as Democratic lawmaker Alexandria Ocasio-Cortez, who questioned Mark Zuckerberg over Facebook's reluctance to police political advertising. Ocasio-Cortez, herself an inspiration, catapulted onto the world's stage following her grassroots campaign that beat a 10-term incumbent by almost 15 percentage points.[15] Her strategy? 'You can't really beat big money with more money,' she says. 'You have to beat them with a totally different game.'[16]

It is no coincidence that her strategy to break old rules paid off. As we will discover, the act of breaking rules is now the standard to achieving success in the future of work. Rules are being rewritten by new leaders who previously may not have taken a stance but are now being hurled into action. This new wave of leadership, of individuals feeling compelled to speak out and make a difference, is radically changing what we know about success. And in certain circumstances, when all else fails, it is often the only way to win.

Leadership from within

This stance against the incumbent hierarchy is not just playing out in politics, it is happening in the workplace too. None more telling of our future than the widespread rebellion of employees in the birthplace of tech, Silicon Valley. Off the back of widespread sexual-abuse allegations against Harvey Weinstein in early October 2017, and the soon-to-follow viral #MeToo movement, over 20,000 Google employees made history on 1 November 2018 by staging a worldwide mass walkout in response to sexual misconduct allegations, gender inequality and systemic racism.[17]

If 20,000 seems like a lot, it is. It is 20 per cent of Google's entire workforce protesting for change. This wildly contradicts the fantasy of 'loving Mondays' that Google tries to promote. It seems that no number of slides or nap pods in the office can make up for poor leadership and bad behaviour, which was allegedly rife among high-powered Google executives. The payoff of nearly $100 million is telling that this behaviour was not uncommon.

In a business made famous by open work culture, the white-wash becomes even more apparent. Just one year following the mass walkout, reports of how senior management was working hard to quell the dissent were being fed to the press in as many channels as could be managed. Top-down enforcement included restricting employees' speech on internal platforms through to the revision of their community guidelines. In some circumstances they went so far as to actively delete employee questions that challenged management in order to silence the internal rebellion.

And yet the rebellion charged on. Driven by the desire for accountability, transparency and decentralization, it was these personal beliefs that were at the core for those who flocked to Silicon Valley in the first place. Upending this would be futile.

The Google walkout was the first step in changing the culture of the tech industry. The act of defiance and questioning authority inspired an entire generation of workers at several other major tech companies including Amazon, Microsoft and Facebook to openly criticize their management and their leadership, creating an open dialogue for change. The hard stance of not being exploited in the workplace has infiltrated the potential for what is possible and led to a new demand to work for ideals we care about. Ironically, the Google corporate mission statement 'to organize the world's information and make it universally accessible and useful' is being used by its employees to make informed decisions about their own workplace and align their values in shaping the world around them. The challenge of information for change led by employees is being radically played out against the challenge of information for profit by its leaders.

With confidence growing among workers in their ability to shape their future, it becomes an obvious next step to ensure there is a future to shape. After Baby Boomers turned a blind eye to climate change, it is now up to the future generation to take matters into their own hands. Inspired by the Google walkout, and surrounded by the effects of delivery of goods and manufacturing, Amazon employees felt this cause was their own. In an open letter to Amazon founder Jeff Bezos and the board of directors signed by 8,702 Amazon employees they asked that the company 'adopt the climate plan shareholder resolution and release a company-wide climate plan that incorporates the principles outlined in this letter. Amazon has the resources and scale to spark the world's imagination and redefine what is possible and necessary to address the climate crisis'.[18]

The Amazon Employees for Climate Justice are active and organized. They openly criticize their own business practices, practices they are all too familiar with. In a previous era, corporate secrets could be maintained more easily as the fear of losing job security was real. But as the false sense of security that a corporate career used to hold fades, so too does the concern for losing one's job. As the balance of power shifts, employees are beginning to understand that if workers themselves are not going to speak out, no one will. They realize that their actions have implications and that they have a responsibility, not necessarily to the company, but for the impact of their actions within that company on the world. As the Amazon Employees for Climate Justice Twitter profile outlines, their belief is that 'it is [their] responsibility to ensure [their] business models don't contribute to the climate crisis'.[19]

This is wholly different from the way big business operated throughout the industrial revolution. Business models and the components of their success were historically derived from their leader, and their leader alone. The ownership of execution is now arguably and demonstrably being led by employees and workers. Mission statements and company visions are being shared, challenged and actively changed through an open dialogue between the few elite leaders and their employees. Now that information is freely available and accessible it is the many that are leading the charge of the few.

In part, this has been made possible by the ability to organize – without the need for union bosses – through social media and developing direct links to the media. It is now possible for workers in the mail room to be heard at the top.

Since the open letter to Bezos in April 2019, change has begun. Most recently Bezos announced a $10 billion donation to his new Earth Fund supporting 'any effort that offers a real possibility to help preserve and protect the natural world'.[20] Rather than the usual public forum announcement made at a global climate change conference with media soaking up his every word, Bezos appropriately chose to announce his news on Instagram, statistically targeting a younger user base in comparison with other social media platforms. Bezos was clear in wanting to address the future generation with his proclamation.

It is this cohort that is fundamental to the changing tactics of future leadership that we explore in this book. A cohort that now has the tools and the momentum to make real change possible.

The image used on Bezo's Instagram post was of the world. The whole Earth as seen from space. In fact, the whole Earth image Bezos chose was almost identical to the whole Earth image Stewart Brand used for his *Whole Earth Catalog* in 1968. Unlikely to be a coincidence.

Unsurprisingly, the Amazon Employees for Climate Justice group issued a statement shortly afterwards applauding the effort of Bezos' philanthropy but continuing to criticize the fact that actual change had still not been made. However, the fact that an open letter arguably bullied one of the richest men in the world to part with 10 per cent of his wealth to address an issue close to the hearts of his employees is monumental.

We have outlined the shift in power and opportunity among workers, but what about those who are not protected by the sanctity of employee benefits?

Job security is a myth

Growing up, the holy grail of my future safety and security could be summarized by getting a full-time job. Dinner table topics among my family covered workplace antics and reinforced the benefits of working in a traditional corporation. With parents who worked for local businesses, securing a job was necessary in raising a young family with four children. I grew up, like many of you, with the understanding that once you had a full-time job you could do anything. That job security is the one thing you can count on in life. A predictable pay-cheque would provide a future where you could buy a house and pay off a mortgage. Where vacationing in a tropical destination could be an annual event. All this supported maintaining the status quo and further instilling the notion that working 9–5 is the backbone to living your best life.

Although I was disenfranchised, the dream to graduate university and become a worker bee came crashing down the hardest for Millennials. Clutching their degrees in hand as they pounded the streets in 2008 only to have job application after job application rejected was soul destroying. Their hopes and dreams, dissipating as the daylight bounced off the concrete onto their first suit, were further crushed as they sat down to watch the evening news headlines of Lehman Brothers and Washington Mutual going bankrupt, which further developed into an international banking crisis with massive bail-outs. Many were still sitting on their parents' sofas having given up the pursuit of employment a year later when the world hit a global economic downturn known as the Great Recession. The worst seen since the financial meltdown of the Great Depression in the 1930s.

As a casualty of this catastrophe I remember all too well the discussions that ensued among widespread redundancies and hire freezes. Being told they could not hire me, not because I was not qualified, but simply because they were not hiring, repeatedly eroded any sense of job security my parents had instilled in me during those dinner table discussions. Being fully qualified with university debt to pay off and zero employment opportunities makes one question the decisions taken to land living back in your parents' basement. Compounded by the fact that without school and work to occupy the mind, there is much more time to think. And many concluded, much like I did, that job security is a lie.

This revelation on a global scale helped to inspire the gig economy, a labour market characterized by the prevalence of short-term contracts or freelance work as opposed to permanent jobs, as we know it today. Although the gig economy has been around for over 100 years, it has become more relevant to our future of work due to the sheer increase in gig workers. By 2030 it is predicted that the number in gig workers will represent over 80 per cent of the global workforce.[21] Its impact is not just felt in our daily lives through the many services they now provide, but is also impacting legislation.[22]

The financial crisis in 2008 was the spark that ignited the fire from the embers of disappointing corporate culture. Since then we have witnessed the gig economy becoming less gig and more economy. Gig workers now account for over one-third of all workers in the United States (approximately 57 million people).[23] Across the pond, the UK has doubled its gig economy workforce in less than two years to 4.7 million workers.[24] If these recent statistics are anything to go by, gig economy workers are becoming the norm.

It is important to note that this exponential rise in gig economy workers is driven by lack of job security rather than apps. Although technology has certainly accelerated the ability to find these gigs, it is not the cause of this shift. In response to these changing times Louis Hyman, professor at the School of Industrial and Labor Relations at Cornell University, claims: 'The history of labour shows that technology does not usually drive social change. On the contrary, social change is typically driven by decisions we make about how to organize our world. Only later does technology swoop in, accelerating and consolidating those changes.'[25]

At its most cynical the gig economy of temporary, flexible jobs done by independent contractors and freelancers means that standard employee benefits that have characterized work for generations are no longer a staple. The risk is now owned by the worker without protection against economic downturns, changing trends and fickle consumer preferences. It can also be argued that career progression can be stifled, and advancement replaced by the next temporary employee willing to do the job cheaper and faster. With a generational workplace mindset built around fair pay and protection, the concept of the gig economy is eroding the traditional system of full-time workers who focus on a lifetime career. It has become a social change, disrupting everything we know about working.

Yet as we have argued throughout this book, change can be a positive thing. And it is happening whether you like it or not, so you might as well get on board. If job security is out the window, then what do we need to work more efficiently, effectively and, potentially most importantly, happily?

What the gig economy has given us in the wake of financial ruin and global economic devastation is ownership and independence. An ability to shape our future, to be our own boss. To lay our individual values and beliefs at the core of whatever gig we choose. It gives us the ability to test a variety of skill sets throughout our lifelong career journey and the agility to move quickly to where our interests and inspirations lie. The world is changing rapidly. If everything will soon be replaced by artificial intelligence and machine learning, then having the good sense to change tack and gain new skills rather than relying on internal management training that is 20 years behind far outweighs the generational model of a one set career path.

Flexibility within the gig economy also supports our desire for equal pay. Minorities secure jobs based on skill set rather than the colour of their skin while working mothers can juggle naptime with consultancy projects. One no longer needs to be in close proximity to the office to access a great job, often a significant barrier in overcoming equal pay at larger corporations where head offices are located in big cities with high rents and even higher costs of living. The gig economy allows freelance and contracting work to be done on the go or based in whatever city you choose. Since Covid-19 hit the world, this now becomes even more relevant as employers begin to accept that not everyone needs to be chained to their desks to work effectively. The pandemic has propelled the gig economy exponentially.

Making the gig economy work for you

The gig economy is not just for unskilled Uber drivers. It has become central to working for some of the smartest thinkers of our time. With flexible hours and the capability to respond to work e-mails on a lounge chair in your own home, it is rare to find even exceptional workers bogged down with the weight of long commutes and bureaucratic performance reviews. Instead, some of our highest performing professionals are participating in the sharing economy, providing their unique skills where and when needed.

The desire to work anywhere and everywhere is felt most by Millennials who have driven the need for flexibility in their lifestyle. In fact, many of them value flexibility over cold hard cash, with 76 per cent of Millennials taking a pay cut to work for a company that offers flexible office hours.[26] It is this generation that has energetically seen the silver lining of the 2008 financial crash and made it work better for them. They prefer to freelance, work flexible hours and collaborate online. With 3 billion new minds coming online within the next 10 years most will never be a full-time employee of a corporation.[27] This is radically different from what we have encountered previously and fundamentally destroys the concrete foundation from which working principles originated.

As we saw with Amazon and Google employees enacting societal and employment change from within, the principle of Joy's Law explains how businesses can tap into the gig economy from the outside. Joy's Law states: 'No matter who you are, most of the smartest people work for someone else.'[28] This is not a blueprint for head-hunters to start chasing talent in other organizations, but instead a manifesto for leaders to tap into networks of smart non-employees based on the fact that the smartest thinkers are rarely caught spinning in the hamster wheel of corporate culture. As we have seen with all the examples outlined in the previous chapters, most notably with Kylie Jenner and Rihanna's business partnerships with Seed Beauty and Fenty Beauty/LVMH respectively, it is this ability to collectively create and execute that has allowed these disruptor businesses to flourish and trounce legacy competition in their sectors.

If Joy's Law provides the framework for tapping into this new, smart, agile and truly global workforce then its leaders need strong collaboration skills to assimilate and acquire. Whereas previous leadership traits were built on managing teams, new leadership suggests that identifying and creating a team is much more important. Becoming a puzzle solver rather than a puzzle maker is a new rule for achieving success in the future of work. This ability to solve puzzles and put the often distinct and diverse pieces together to create a winning whole is what sets a rebellious leader apart. There is no book on the subject (until now) and this concept is not taught at business school. And yet this concept is one with which we all have grown up in the sandbox at an early age, learning that 'two heads are better than one'. It seems this advice is finally catching on.

Replacing dictatorial leadership is new leadership which abolishes authority and welcomes collaboration. It is important to recognize that this does not only exist in the gig economy.

This concept of true collaboration exists with full-time employees as well. In short, no matter where and how you are working, you are no longer the smartest person in the room. The people you collaborate with are no longer your employed minions, they are contributing their skills and their time to your cause. You do not lead them, they lead you. You do not fire them, they fire you. Trust becomes the cornerstone of building a business where hidden agendas and hierarchies die. When trust is eroded, employees step up to take action, as illustrated by Amazon and Google employees alike.

As this concept plays out in business, we cannot ignore the monopolistic influence of technology companies and their power over our way of life. This is now more apparent than ever before. Their survival is based on surveillance and, like the big banks that became the villains of our economy, their enormity makes them difficult to police as they use significant lobbying muscle to avoid regulation. It is also becoming harder to ignore the fact that these big tech companies are commoditizing us. That our choices, our decisions and our online actions are the raw materials in these intangible products that are being sold and resold for profit. It is the harvesting of our data that is being monetized at auction to the highest bidder. This concept is no longer one of which we are pleased to be a part and the fight against the 'doing well' of the financially driven Silicon Valley of today has begun.

If we go back to basics with Brand's original principle that computers can become tools for good, we first need to understand what it is that we as a generation care about. With previous leadership tools and management styles eroding in the future of work, it becomes necessary to look at how we inspire greatness through a different form of leadership. But to inspire we must first identify the areas that motivate us.

As seen with the Google walkouts and Amazon petitions, the promise of a pay-cheque is no longer a key motivator for employees. We have also proven with Kylie Jenner and Kylie Cosmetics that you no longer need 50 years' experience in a sector to revolutionize it. With old rules thrown out the window, it is time to start considering what it is we care about. What are the new rules we need to put in place to ensure our success in the future of work?

Greed is... gone?

Starting the year off right is something we all aim for. Reflecting on the previous year in a food coma of leftover turkey watching reruns of *Friends*, we tend to hit the ground running on the first of January. It is an important day filled with promise and hope for the year ahead. A day to announce future plans. As such, it was no coincidence that it was on this day in 2020 that one of the most senior Twitter executives in London made a big announcement. The announcement was not the expected plans for the company in the year ahead, but instead that he quit. On his Twitter account @BruceDaisley tweeted: 'This week I reached a milestone of eight years at Twitter. I decided it's time for a change... so today was my last day.'[29]

The fact that this statement was made by someone in the most senior of positions at one of the largest tech companies in the world on the first of January is exceptionally telling. The announcement was not only timely but, I argue, quite indicative of what the future holds. Rather than kicking the year off with profitability charts and strategic global plan announcements, individuals are coming out of holiday reflection with insight into their personal values rather than what they are planning to do for the company they work for.

This has a domino effect. We are seeing others, like Daisley, not just thinking about the alignment of their life, but actually actioning it. This bold action is beginning to instil confidence within ourselves to also take the leap into work that aligns with our beliefs. More people are questioning their commitment to their current job and actively looking at what else is out there.

Again, with the impact of Covid-19 as employees have been furloughed and many have lost their jobs, the entire employment culture has been re-evaluating what is important to them moving forward.

Daisley has been on a similar journey to the rest of us, questioning whether his work aligns to his passion. He launched his exceptionally popular podcast *Eat Sleep Work Repeat* in 2017 speaking to scientists and experts on how to improve jobs. He followed up his findings by publishing the *Sunday Times* business bestseller *The Joy of Work* in 2019, which outlines a series of ways to 'fix your work culture and fall in love with your job again', including thirty hacks to get more joy from our burnt-out, uninspired work lives. The book is proving to be just as popular as he taps into the zeitgeist of how much of the modern world feels about their working lives. A fact, it seems, that not even the apparently satisfied top Twitter executive could escape.

With many of us spending at least three days a week in meetings, Daisley facetiously argues that if 'a child's brain was transported into ours and they saw what happened in those meetings, they'd say "you spent three days a week in meetings pretending to pay attention"'.[30] It is this link to our childhood, to our base instincts and understanding, that makes this statement so poignant. Daisley goes on to argue that our use of technology as a tool for advancement has created a horrible operating system for modern work that is permeated by misdirection and lies. In fact, we have created a work life that we hate. That our current work structures foster feelings of being unfulfilled, leaving us feeling anxious and insecure. Daisley goes on to argue that to any outsider this working structure clearly does not work, but that over time our resistance erodes and we submit to it because we feel there is no other way.

But that sentiment is changing.

As we have outlined previously with the Amazon Employees for Climate Justice organization, employees are beginning to make a direct link between their day-to-day actions in their working lives and their individual values. Differing from the past where the top-down hierarchy left little to influence, they make their involvement as active, now participating in the products and services that the company delivers. When that company does not align to their personal values, employees are speaking out rather than cashing in. Employees want to feel that the organization they work for, and their role within that organization, contributes to a better world. Armed with the tools to organize and make change, they want to act.

While running my agency I noticed this shift in my employees when choosing which clients to work with. As part of my desire to collaborate, my employees were always involved with the decision process of taking on new clients and the accounts they wanted to work on. Over six years I noticed a distinct change in what got them out of bed in the morning. Instead of tripping over each other to run sponsorship sales for the hedonistic music festivals we launched the agency with, they began to vie for projects with a sustainability angle. By comparison, in the first two years less than 10 per cent of our clients were purpose-driven, but by 2016, just six years after launching, our cause-related clients made up over 50 per cent of the business. Compared with other agencies we had substantially more purpose-led projects because we did not solely focus on sports sponsorship – a direct reflection of our Millennial staff's input.

According to Deloitte's *Global Millennial Survey 2019* based on 13,416 Millennials across 42 countries and territories, 76 per cent of Millennials view business as a source of powerful and positive social impact. Understandably, trust in the media is low among this cohort, with even lower opinions of political and religious leadership. This scepticism and lack of visible leadership are the momentum needed to kickstart real change. No longer expecting change to come from the powers that be, the new generation of leaders is making change happen for themselves. This need for change is so great that 'they were also more attracted to making a positive impact in their communities or society at large (46 per cent) than having children and starting families (39 per cent)'.[31]

An extreme departure from the 'greed is good' mantra of the eighties, the new generation is putting their money where their mouth is. According to Fidelity Investments' *Evaluate a Job Offer Study*, Millennials would be willing to take a $7,600 pay cut for a better quality of work life.[32] Further research from LinkedIn discovered that nearly 9 out of 10 Millennials would take a pay cut to work at a company whose mission and values aligned with their own.[33] This cannot be overlooked as a fad. This is a radical shift in ideologies among one of the largest working cohorts of our time. Their expectation weighs heavily on the leaders they look towards and will eventually become.

It is this new drive of aligning values to business that has seen marketing communications stray from a focus on features and benefits, to one of mission statements. Simon Sinek's book *Start with Why* beautifully articulates this as a key distinction of what makes businesses successful now with his 'golden circle' theory.[34] The theory states that business value propositions that start with the purpose of the business, rather than what it has achieved or what it does resonate better with consumers' reasoning behind the purchase of a product. By telling customers why your business exists they can more easily and more readily make purchasing decisions by aligning their own values to those of your business.

What Sinek does not outline is why the golden circle works better for organizations now compared with previous generations. The generational differences in relation to core values are significant. Where patriotism is fundamental to Traditionalists, Generation X values informality. Where Baby Boomers value anti-war, Millennials march for diversity.[35] This has never been more apparent than the summer of 2020 during worldwide Black Lives Matter protests.

After generations of dissonance between big business drivers and individual motivations, we now have a desire to go back to basics and align what happens in our world with our personal output and engagement within it. It is hoped this shifting impact on work and leadership will drive future generations farther. We have seen first-hand the outcome of the 'greed is good' mantra of the Baby Boomer generation. The fixation a generation has had on driving up the stock price has left a gap in some fundamental principles such as our planet and social justice. The pendulum has begun to swing. As d'Ancona puts it: 'Real generation gaps come along once every few decades and this gap is significant.'

Today's youth are inspiring in the way that they see the world, vastly different from the way previous generations have seen the world. No longer mesmerized by old capitalist orders, they intuit that they will have a lot of work to do when it comes time to run the show. D'Ancona further argues:

> The previous couple of generations left so much undone and failed to step up to the plate. The end of the Cold War in 1989 and the crash of 2008 were two obvious opportunities to reset, but neither was seized. I sense real change coming, though it is hard to say exactly what it will be like and whether it will be – as one hopes – properly thought through.

D'Ancona's viewpoint is inherently felt within the next generation. A subtle bubbling underneath the surface that change is coming. But it is *how* we execute that change that is critical.

Replacing greed is a greater understanding of boundaries, which is ironic given that this book is about our potential to demolish them. But it is the boundaries that exist with our planet's resources and within ourselves that we must navigate. Understanding this, in Daisley's tweet announcing his departure from Twitter, he also added: 'If anyone is doing anything to fight climate change and wants someone to help them for free PLEASE hit me up.'

From the seedlings of the idea that information is a window for opportunity with Stewart Brand to the current struggle with basic social values, we have witnessed almost a century of friction between doing well and doing good. It has become a battle of ideologies originating from the few of the past to the many of the future. This book argues that a generation's focus on this friction has created a lack of progress for what we really want, or more importantly, what we really need.

The following chapters look towards the present. Let us focus on execution and uncover what new rules we must follow to help us actively lead this change. But I must warn you, this type of leadership needs a bit of rebellion, so it is best we start off with a drink. Specifically, a craft beer.

PART TWO

The Present

CHAPTER FOUR

Replacing the C-suite

Punk leadership drives the craft beer revolution

James Watt is often seen wearing a newsboy cap, quite apt given that Watt is a man who likes to make headlines. As one of the co-founders of BrewDog, a multinational brewery and pub chain which describes itself as a 'post-punk, apocalyptic, mother****** of a craft brewery',[1] his responsibility for the beer brand's strategy and marketing has seen them gain traction through controversy. Media antics have included selling a range of bottled beers stuffed with dead animals; driving a tank down Camden High Street in London; naming a beer after the heroin-and-cocaine cocktail that killed River Phoenix and John Belushi; employing a dwarf to petition the British government for the introduction of a two-thirds pint glass; and projecting naked images of the BrewDog co-founders onto the Houses of Parliament.

BrewDog's revolution manifesto, which can be found on their website, states:

> We are not afraid. Not of revolution. Not of challenging the status quo. We will do whatever it takes, beer in hand, to obliterate mass-produced, tasteless, monolithic beer.[2]

Their press stunts drove awareness quickly, but Watt argues that it is their authenticity and belief system that has projected their meteoric rise from a shed on an industrial estate in north-east Scotland to one of the fastest-growing drinks companies, globally employing over 1,000 people, with a company valuation of $2 billion in 2020.[3]

Watt's unique approach to business is credited in part to his unorthodox work experience prior to launching BrewDog with his school friend Martin Dickie. Unlike his fellow law students, Watt took to the high seas after graduating where he became captain of a deep-sea trawler, a profession that runs in his family. Being at sea two weeks out of every four, Watt and Dickie spent their spare time making beer. It got so good that whisky writer Michael Jackson told them to give up their day jobs after tasting it.[4] Which they did, founding the company in 2007. Watt was just 24 years old. By 2009 they had purchased their first bar and by the end of 2018 they operated 78 bars worldwide. The rest, as they say, is history.

Their fast entry onto the stagnant stage of the beer industry was truly revolutionary, single-handedly driving the craft brewery movement on a global scale. Alongside their awards for beer, Watt also gained a reputation for his leadership achievements, winning Entrepreneur of the Year awards at both the Prince's Scottish Youth Business Trust and the National Business Awards for Scotland in 2008.[5]

In 2015 Watt outlined his approach to business in his first book *Business for Punks: Break all the rules – the BrewDog way*. It proclaims to be the 'business bible for a new generation' and provides advice including 'Your brand is not yours' and 'Networking is for fools'.[6] A book filled with practical advice dispersed with new thinking and based on breaking all the rules. Underneath this rebellious attitude is the core message that for a business to succeed you need to know what you stand for.

In November 2019 I was asked to pitch to a room of buyers at a drinks industry conference in London, presenting my own independent brand of Canadian ice wine, REBEL Pi. Arriving at the conference early, I had time to kill and chose to sit in on a keynote session which had Watt being interviewed by a magazine editor to discuss his journey – a speaking scenario I assume has been well rehearsed. Wearing Doc Martens and an oat-coloured newsboy cap, what struck me, aside from his say-it-like-it-is manner and strong Scottish accent, was his response to the question: 'What is the worst piece of advice you have ever received?' to which Watt deadpanned: 'Getting advice.'

Watt went on to explain that as a new business that did things differently, the advice from seasoned professionals was useless and irrelevant. BrewDog's approach to success was built on different constraints, with a different set of rules. What worked for drinks industry professionals and so-called mentors during a time when monolithic beer companies ruled the roost would not work for BrewDog today.

This flies in the face of almost everything we have come to understand about experience. Is experience not knowledge? And if so, would it not be wise to seek advice so that you do not make the same mistakes? The assumption is that by taking advice from those with more experience you will be empowered to achieve success quicker. You will not fall into the traps that previously ensnared other leaders. You will be one step ahead.

This assumption of listening to our elders as a method for success is ingrained in us by the time we can crawl. Our parents raise us to put faith in the fact that they know what they are doing, because after all, they successfully made it to adulthood. It is not until the rebellious teenage years that we start questioning whether our parents' path should be our own path. If their rules should be our rules.

In business today there is less room for this type of trial and error. Too much is on the line for us to take time to test out theories. Therefore, we understandably fall back on the general principle that mentorship and advice are beneficial. This route is much easier than trying to figure it out ourselves.

And like others before them, this is what the young BrewDog founders did initially. It was indeed this very action to seek feedback which launched the business in the first place after the compliment paid by Jackson. Idealistic and enthusiastic, they took the advice given, implementing it with both the speed and agility you often find with start-ups. Fortunately, it was this quick implementation which provided immediate feedback, which was that the advice provided was quite bad advice indeed. It is no surprise that in his book Watt outlines:

> My advice, to those seeking advice, is don't even bother. You need to be driven and know your own way... You know where you're going and how you get there is up to you. Other people don't understand, and they certainly don't care as much as you do. A patchwork quilt of other people's half-baked ideas is a recipe for nothing but disaster. Don't follow but lead.

As a fellow entrepreneur who had minimal work experience under my belt before I launched my first business, this resonated with me. Following my success my business choices were often discussed in the context of what was provided to me. Did I have mentors? How did I know what to do? Who did I look to for guidance in growing?

The reality is no one. I had arrived in London with nothing but a backpack and some cash in my pocket. If it wasn't the time difference between London and my family in Canada that stopped me from asking for help it was the fact that they all loved working in their corporate careers without any experience of starting a business. My network of senior professionals that I knew, let alone could ask for advice, was non-existent. At the time I remember thinking launching a business without a mentor was foolish and irresponsible. In hindsight, I believe it is what led to my success early on.

In the previous chapter we explored how the foundation of tension between doing good and doing well has inspired people into action. Employees are speaking out; rebel leaders are emerging. The generational values of what we held dear in both our personal and professional lives have shifted dramatically compared with those values of future generations. This is all bolstered by the feeling that everything is now possible through digital technology. Having witnessed the failings of democracy in a digital age and uncovered the exploitation of digital tools by big business to manage the masses, we are now ready to do something about both.

In this chapter we are going to look at what the future of work will become as new leadership begins to take shape. Specifically, we will outline the new rules of engagement and what actions leaders need to take to wake up the disenfranchised. We know it does not have to be the way it has always been. Rebel businesses, political and social leaders are proving that change can happen.

But how can we make this change for ourselves and the world around us? How can we break the rigidity of rules that are bound into our current methods of work?

In order to answer these tough questions, we must redefine what we know about leadership and focus on discovering the values people hold most dear.

New managers become new leaders

Not seeking advice is radical advice. Especially as we have grown up with the idea that our elders are who we need to learn from.

Although this concept has existed since the time of the hunter-gatherer, as we reflected upon earlier when identifying patterns of behaviour and trust, the concept of receiving sage advice is a relatively new term in relation to business, advancement and, as we will soon explore, leadership.

The catchall term 'mentorship' is used to describe this transfer of 'knowledge from a more experienced or more knowledgeable person to help guide a less experienced or less knowledgeable person'.[7] The use of mentorship programmes was in part driven by senior executives as a way to illustrate seniority while sharing one's knowledge. These became popular discussions in the 1980s. By the mid-1990s 'mentorship' had become part of everyday business terminology. But it was not until the 21st century that the term 'mentee' became widespread, driven by the United States to address systemic racism and gender bias in the workplace. During this time, becoming a role model (also made popular during this period) was the holy grail of what defined individuals as true leaders.

It is interesting therefore to realize that the principle of mentorship, or providing seasoned advice to those starting out, was popularized not because of its effectiveness but because it became a tagline for a wider-scale corporate communications campaign in North America. A communications campaign that became an effective tool for current leaders to propel themselves farther up the corporate ladder in an effort to appear to be giving back to those they managed below. Upon further investigation of leadership books written in the 21st century, it becomes glaringly obvious that the outcome of such mentorship is not actually discussed, nor any case studies to their effectiveness. Instead the literature is often written by leaders and CEOs outlining their own methods of mentorship. A step-by-step guide on how to mentor staff, practical guidance on how to help people get ahead. Whether those proposed methods worked or not is never part of the story.

Understandably so because the concept of mentorship is big business. It makes sense to cash in on what you know, rather than spend time and money fact-checking results. A quick Amazon search will pull up over 1,000 books on mentorship and of those focussed on business mentorship currently available, there are surprisingly only three books about actually being mentored. *The Mentee's Guide*[8] is written by an 'expert on mentoring', while *Mentee's Guide: How to have a successful relationship with a mentor*[9] and *Making the Most of Being Mentored: How to grow from a mentoring partnership*[10] are books written by academics. Shockingly that means that just 0.3 per cent of all books on mentorship discuss the process as a success from a mentee's perspective.

And Watt is not alone in rejecting the mentor concept. Elon Musk who epitomizes paving new paths is also known for rejecting mentorship, stating:

> I don't have a mentor, though I do try and get feedback from as many people as possible. I have friends and I ask them what they think of this, that and the other thing... I think it's good to solicit feedback, particularly negative feedback actually.[11]

The realization that the concept of mentorship is a smokescreen to prop up outdated concepts of leadership and old rules of business further outlines the benefit of democratizing information that we explored in Chapter 3. However, in this case, it relates to the illusion of achieving career progression.

Therefore, if everything we have learned about leadership is not for the benefit of future leaders, but instead to bolster those few already in positions of power, it remains that we must redefine leadership as it exists today. Old paths were built with old rules. They reinforced the hierarchical business structures required to mass produce. They were necessary to keep everyone in check and helped to churn out products on the production line. But the world is no longer the same. We now require flexibility, the antithesis of any industrial revolution. Therefore, old rules no longer apply.

So, if we are to start anew, then it makes sense to start off right. With new rules. Rules that make sense and are underpinned by the strength of our values and beliefs. The act of breaking old rules then becomes less an act of defiance; instead, an act of necessity for growth to happen. *Rule breaking is now a requirement for progress.*

This is not to say that we should throw the baby out with the bathwater. As the previous chapters have outlined, there are many historical influences and significant advancements that need to be considered to move forward more effectively. Unlike the leap Silicon Valley initially made to 'move fast and break things' we need instead to reset and strategically plan for our future from past learnings. There is no better place to start assembling our future of work than by assessing those that will be stepping up to redefine it – our future leaders.

We have outlined how the demographic and societal changes of the past 50 years have created a shift in the way we live, the way we think and the way we work. Those foundations are now prime drivers in the way we lead. They are critical in determining our business success and relevant for the century to come.

It is important to acknowledge at this stage that although we identify only a selection of new leaders in this book, they represent a cohort of changing ideals reflecting a generation of new leadership and new thinking. Their commonalities in the way they have gained success are based on new rules that have gained momentum among us all, but none more prominent than Millennials.

Currently Millennials are the world's most populous generation and by 2025 Millennials will represent 75 per cent of the global workforce. Based on numbers alone, the growth in the number of Millennials is being driven by developing countries, with nearly 9 in every 10 living in an emerging economy such as China and India.[12] With the world growing ever smaller through the advances of technology, this cannot be overlooked.

The three core values of leadership

Value 1: Positive change

As we saw in the previous chapter, making a positive difference and doing good in the world is incredibly important to Millennials and undoubtedly also for the future generations to come. By comparison 62 per cent of Millennials cite this as a key driver for the businesses they work for compared with 52 per cent in Generation X. What makes this statistic unique, aside from the growing importance of doing good, is that there is a rise in awareness of individual actions, with 55 per cent of Millennials caring about what their family and friends think about their career compared with just 43 per cent of the previous generation.[13]

New for this generation is social media, which provides the ability to share our lives beyond our immediate communities. This larger audience makes us hyper-aware of our actions and our image. At its most negative, social media has driven self-conscious anxiety and doubt with overused filters selling unrealistic goals and expectations. At its most positive, as we explored in Chapter 2, social media gives us the opportunity to be in control of the images, attitudes and values that influence our everyday lives. We are responsible for the content we put out. This management over individual influence gives us power. Power to live more authentically and the ability to then communicate this authenticity to the world.

With work consuming one-third of our lives, this impact on living authentically is exceptionally relevant. Our insatiable appetite to share our lives means that work, which makes up half our awake time, plays a feature role in our social media feed. It would then feel inauthentic to project images that reflect inaccurate values of how we truly feel.

Further than just the feeling of being fake, projecting images that do not reflect how we feel creates psychological stress known as cognitive dissonance. This stress exists when our actions and ideas are not psychologically consistent with our thoughts or feelings. When this happens, the theory states that people will do everything in their power to change their situation until it becomes congruent.[14]

Before social media it was easier to reduce cognitive dissonance between the job you did and the values you held because your justification was internalized. You could easily justify being employed by an organization that was against your values by changing the conflicting cognition in your head, such as 'I need to put food on the table for my family', or through new behaviours or cognitions that had nothing to do with your work environment such as volunteering at the local soup kitchen. And many just used plain denial, telling themselves, 'My organization isn't that bad, they have a CSR programme.' Unfortunately, utilizing these methods to reduce cognitive dissonance is no longer an option when we actively promote our activities online for the rest of the world to see. Put simply, we are more aware when our actions do not line up with our values because we are constantly reminded of our actions as we upload them onto our social media feeds. This update becomes a continual stream of conscious engagement with our network. You cannot as easily hide your actions when you are sharing them daily. Therefore, the only option remaining to reduce our cognitive dissonance and stress when our actions do not align with our values is to completely change the behaviour itself: 'I will no longer work for this organization.'

It can therefore be argued that future generations of leaders may hold similar values to those of previous generations, but there are structural and environmental crossroads that exist now that require leaders and individuals to hold values with more rigour. Their values are no longer just ideological but forced through action as a means of aligning our social media feeds with our true selves. In simple terms, the importance of living authentically is no longer a slogan for your Instagram feed, but a physiological state of necessity driven by technology.

Value 2: Work–life balance

The phrase 'achieving work–life balance' was first used in the UK in the late 1970s, but has taken on a new meaning with the technological changes that make it possible for workers to stay in touch 24 hours a day, seven days a week. Not only does the 'always-on' generation want an opportunity to switch off, the post-pandemic generation needs to build boundaries as their office and home lives blur. As jobs undergo radical transformation to fit the new norm, two jobs that are lagging behind are journalist and stockbroker, both making the list for the top 10 worst jobs for work–life balance, according to the *Huffington Post*.[15] To understand this shift in work–life balance and what it means in the future of work, I spoke to a man who has made his career doing both.

Cory Johnson started his career founding financial news website TheStreet (with CNBC star Jim Cramer) in his native New York City, but was eventually lured to Silicon Valley in 1998 at the height of the dot-com bubble. It has given him a unique perspective. Recalling his time in finance he told me:

> There were years and years when I went to work before the sun came up and went home only after the sun went down. That's how we do in finance and that's how we do in New York. And that could be a reason you don't see a lot of 50-year-old people in finance – that pace burns you out and destroys your relationship with your family.[16]

As he moved away from finance into journalism, Johnson continued this pace to get the inside scoop. He tells me of his drive to be the first, always on the ground, always at the right place at the right time. He recalls thinking that the only way to beat the competition every single day was to be 'always on', around the clock. For a man from 'the city that never sleeps' it was the only thing he knew.

And this relentless pace worked. As a journalist, he interviewed everyone from Steve Jobs to Michael Jordan to Bill Gates. He publicly feuded with Carly Fiorina and Elon Musk. He watched as companies like Facebook and Google grew from college projects to become the biggest companies in the world. And later in his life, as a hedge fund manager and venture investor, Johnson got inside some of those very companies to see what makes them tick and how they work. But eventually the effects of that relentless pace took their toll.

Early one Sunday morning in 2008, Johnson was ducking out of the house on his way to the office. His wife and toddler were fast asleep. The sun was just coming up over the hills east of San Francisco and he heard his one-year-old wake and start to whimper. 'I went to pick her up out of her crib and she freaked out,' he says. 'She wasn't crying anymore, she was now screaming. She looked at me with no recognition at all. She was terrified and had no idea who I was – my own daughter – she had no idea.'

Johnson realized that as he worked around the clock, making more money than he had ever imagined, he had abandoned his newborn. 'I hadn't been on a plane, I hadn't been out of town,' he says. 'I just hadn't seen her in five weeks.'

As his career took off in Silicon Valley, he noticed a more holistic way of working compared with New York. 'People here work hard, but they work smart,' he says. 'There's a lot of attention paid to energy, bringing your best to every opportunity.' He saw Steve Jobs taking regular walking meetings (a practice Johnson deployed for years while anchoring Bloomberg West

TV). He took note of LinkedIn CEO Jeff Weiner insisting that his schedule had hours a day blocked off for nothing but thinking time. He saw the hard-charging software CEO Tom Siebel regularly taking time out to kiteboard or go hunting (albeit ferried about on his private jet).

'People in New York want money,' he says. 'People in Silicon Valley want it all: money, achievement, family, health, technological advancement, athletic achievement... all of it! And they get it. All.'

Johnson has since rededicated himself to his family, trying to achieve greater work–life balance. And his daughters? 'They know me!' he says. 'They talk to me every day, and they're teenagers!'

This is a common story and reflects how old rules are negatively affecting not only our potential but our lives and relationships. Where old rules in the workplace rewarded time spent in the office, which often reinforced pay gaps and inequalities, new rules argue that productivity is greater with greater flexibility. Rather than being married to your job, you now fit your job around your marriage. Like Johnson, you can now make time for your children while still having a high-flying career.

A long list of recent studies has proven the value and virtues of flexible working and specific studies show that those nine-to-fivers waste a significant amount of time during their day.[17] By providing flexibility on when tasks are done, productivity and performance increase. But studies and flowcharts are not needed for our new generation of leader. They already know this. These studies and flowcharts are not for the future, they are for the past. They are used to try to convince the older generation who suffered in silence with long hours in the office that working from home is a good thing (despite being forced to work at home during a pandemic, most probably still do not agree). You will never see a Millennial or Generation Z write a blog about the benefits of working from home, they already know the benefits – and are doing it. Therefore there is a lot of time spent talking about a form of working that people are already championing (new generation) or people abhor (older generation). And much of it is time and effort spent trying to convince those who cannot be convinced. Ironically, there is a lot of time wasted talking about time wasted. Covid-19 has further widened this gap and while a younger generation was able to swiftly move into this transition, the older generation is being forced to play catch-up.

The 'always-on' generation is descriptively just that. Rather than discussing the benefits of working flexibly the new role of a human resources director is about getting the future generation to be always on about their work. And that is not about workplace perks and benefits. It is about people being passionate about what they are doing. By shifting the focus away from discussing the benefits of working from home and realizing that a passionate employee is not just working from home, they are working from *everywhere*. This shifts the conversation, and that changes the business.

Work–life balance not only creates a more productive workforce, it also shifts the power away from hiring the stagnant pool of the pale, male, stale we have grown up with.

A 2019 LinkedIn study found that 82 per cent of parents were in pursuit of flexible work. These parents were wanting to work from home at least one day per week, enabling women to continue their careers and at the same time providing men the ability to support in the home, effectively balancing equal opportunities for both genders.[18] But it is not just parents who benefit; flexible working provides opportunities for other pay gaps to close including socio-economic and disability pay gaps. Although less tracked than gender pay gaps, these are gaps to pay attention to. While an average gap between what non-disabled and disabled workers earn is 13.6 per cent, when combined with socio-economic figures it shows that disabled men from the Bangladeshi community in Britain experience a staggering pay gap of 56 per cent.[19] Flexible working will not eradicate these issues, but it does help to alleviate some of the structural inequalities facing these groups, including accessing public transport and blatant racism in the workplace.

The point of doing this is not just to do good or do better for all people in the hope of achieving some Mother Teresa status in business. Instead it is based on driving greater profitability and building businesses beyond their legacy boundaries. This can only be done with diversity – diversity of thinking, of experience, of skill set. A study by *Harvard Business Review* that looked at diversity in leadership functions found that diverse companies were significantly more innovative than their non-diverse counterparts. Specifically organizations that had leadership diversity acquired through experience and had inherent diversity through gender, ethnicity and sexual orientation were 45 per cent more likely to report that their firm's market share grew over the previous year and were 70 per cent more likely to report the firm captured a new market.[20]

This highlights significant benefits and further proves that potential in business has not yet reached its peak. And all with a small change to provide a bit of work–life balance.

Value 3: Connect in a meaningful way

Generational leadership differences arise not just in the execution of leadership itself but in the perception of what these generations think a leader looks like. Baby Boomers and Generation Xers identify with leaders who are culture beacons and role models respectively.[21] Admired from a distance, leadership is associated by these older generations with 'strength', with leaders often defined as individuals who show up to lead during critical moments. Workers from this generation see leaders as ones who support an organization during difficult transitions, within the business or through challenging economic times. Often, they view leaders as a single reference point, a north star, for an organization in chaos.

This viewpoint of leadership being singular is due to the centuries-old siloed nature of business structures. With only one person at the top commanding the ship, there is really only one person to attribute organizational leadership to. Furthermore, this command and control style means that information flow from the top down ensures that the leader at the top directs who is in the 'need to know'. Baby Boomers and Generation Xers only have one leader because they only see and hear one leader. Their acceptance of what leadership should look like is skewed because that is all they have been given. In an isolated environment this works to keep everyone towing the line.

However, we no longer work in silos. No one knows this more than Millennials, which is why their perception of what a leader looks like is quite different. Instead of the single role model so actively used in the nineties, Millennials have more options. They are exposed to more people and examples of leadership beyond the confines of their office cubicle. In a study that analysed over 267,000 employee comments it was discovered that Millennials most commonly associate the word 'connectors' with the term 'leader'. They see leaders as collaborators, 'people who connect diverse workforces to a common purpose, have their employees' long-term growth and personal interests in mind and show up during critical moments in their personal life or career'.[22] It is this view of leadership as part of both their personal and professional lives which provides the act of leadership to come in a variety of forms. Rather than aligning to a single leader, the future generation is able to turn to myriad leaders in all aspects of their lives to push them beyond their boundaries. They amalgamate leadership traits like a puzzle to support their unique viewpoint on the world and in their work.

Contrasting to previous generations, collaborative leadership aims to break down silos in the workplace so that information is shared organically, and everyone takes responsibility for the whole. Where historically formal hierarchies and robust structures thrived, current generations value the agility that flatter organizational structures provide. As we explored in previous pages, the illusion of job security is no longer confining the future generation to adhere to rigid top-down management. Instead, collaboration and continued learning are key to success in the workplace.

Furthermore, the fact that our future leaders are digital natives and have grown up in a world with infinite information at their fingertips means they know first-hand that no one person has all the answers. They are adept at integrating knowledge and curating this information to shape their individuality. This ability is now being utilized in their approach to leadership and business functions. In the way that their experience assimilating information online is vastly superior to any generation before them, so too is their ability to collaborate.

As a rebel leader I use this to my advantage. I am often found actively, and often aggressively, asking questions and searching for answers in an aim to collaborate. My curiosity now knows no bounds as I am filled with endless opportunities to connect with people beyond the boundaries of my home office. When I wanted to launch a wine brand I did not undertake a winemaking course or apprentice at the nearest vineyard; instead I collaborated with the best winemaker in the area to tap into their longstanding experience to produce my vision. I know how to focus on my strengths and collaborate on my weaknesses. This enables me to do more, and to do it sooner, better and quicker.

The desire for collaboration and connectiveness can also be seen in the latest start-ups such as Airbnb, Lyft and Uber, all taking advantage of the sharing economy. It is this generation who understands that strong networks are a requirement in both business and life.

These generational leadership differences are vast and are already shaping the future of work. The old rule book is being ripped up and replaced with an ever-evolving digital playbook that is constantly iterated upon, not just by the new C-suite leaders but by everyone in true collaborative style. This iteration continually drives these values forward and looks for ways to improve. It is Brailsford's marginal gains theory on steroids and played out on a global stage in business. Fortunately, we are all reaping the benefits.

HUMAN CONNECTION IN A DIGITAL WORLD

These core values are being driven through new leaders because connectiveness is fundamentally human. As our lives become more digitally driven, we now have the capability to become more connected. Capitalizing on this new reality are social media networks. But more is not always better.

As we explored in Chapter 3, the friction between doing good and doing well has exploited our inherent need for human connection so much so that we are selling ourselves and our privacy for an extra 'like' or 'follow'. Although purpose has begun to drive many industries – such as the desire to see more sustainability in fashion or healthier food in take-away services – it has yet to infiltrate the social network organizations that are replacing our offline connectivity. Although we are more connected than ever, some of the loneliest people are those who have more online-only friends, proving that while connecting to others is intrinsically important it is the *meaningfulness* of those connections that is more relevant.

As the novelty of creating online connections wears off, people are becoming aware that greater connections can also create greater isolation and are on a mission to address this. Born in Saudi Arabia, Fahad Saud is one such man on a mission. A traveller at heart, he left the dramatic mountaintops and endless sand dunes of his homeland at the young age of 18 in 2008. Spending time in Paris and Miami before eventually landing in New York City to attend university he remembers using social media to maintain the connections he made during his travels. As a digital native he was the first to jump on any new platform and shared everything, reflecting on that time as being a bit of an 'oversharer'. His use of social media was significant, driving his online networks to grow exponentially with 100,000+ connections at the start of 2015, a substantial following at that time. But by the summer of that year he had deleted everything.

What drove this social media lover to erase his entire online presence in less than two years? Saud told me:

> I struggled to replicate the boundaries I had in my offline relationships online. I overshared everything that went on in my life and, over time, it began to affect my relationships with friends and family members negatively. They would see me out when I wasn't supposed to be out or doing things they didn't agree with. It began to seed doubt in everything I was doing and made me feel like the people that I was closest to no longer understood me. But growing my following made me feel good and so I continued. However, being in my early twenties trying to create my identity with this layer of doubt eventually became debilitating, I was riddled with anxiety. I felt I had no choice but to delete everything.[23]

Saud eventually re-engaged in order to re-establish communications with the people he cared about but set out to ensure it would not affect him negatively again. With self-imposed rules in place he felt he could manage his social media in a way that would not affect his mental health. A key rule was to keep his accounts private and refrain from oversharing. He wanted to create small spaces, private places for him to share appropriate content based on the group or the platform he was using. But his activity went against the addictive nature that the social media networks are built on. Predictably his self-imposed rules for small, private spaces failed and as time went on, old habits came back. This is unsurprising; these platforms were designed this way. They were built to be highly addictive because the more people engage, the higher the business's valuation becomes.

Napster founder and early Facebook investor Sean Parker provides insight into the workings of these social media behemoths, stating: 'It's a social-validation feedback loop... exactly the kind of thing that a hacker like myself would come up with, because you're exploiting a vulnerability in human psychology.'[24]

These platforms are designed to consume all your time and attention. Social media is not something you can partake of in moderation. This is often why you find yourself scrolling through your feeds in the middle of the night rather than catching up on much needed sleep. Like anything addictive, the entire experience is designed to compel you to seek rewarding stimuli in the form of validation, whether that be from family, friends or strangers. Every notification, app icon and touchscreen gesture has been carefully orchestrated to ensure maximum enticement. Each action has been moderated and researched through countless data points, but it is only recently that the same level of focus has been devoted to looking at the adverse consequences of our consumption.

Saud's experience of feeling more isolated despite a growing online network is more common than one would expect, and it seems the younger the generation, the worse it gets. A recent study into loneliness revealed that 40 per cent of people aged 16–24 feel lonely often or very often.[25] Despite the ability of social media to facilitate more effective communications with others, it does not necessarily provide better relationships. It seems the more online connections we have, the more isolated we feel. This is not technology's fault; it lies in the structure of our brains.

Oxford University anthropologist and psychologist Robin Dunbar made a surprising discovery about human connections and the size of our brains when trying to understand primate grooming. He discovered that the size of an animal's neocortex predicts the group size it can assimilate into. Applying his research to humans, he was able to calculate that the human brain can only optimally manage a network of 150 connections, a theory that is now widely used in management tactics today. As social media has become the new normal this theory has been challenged by researchers over time, but the results have remained stable.[26] Despite our ability to connect with thousands of people online, it seems we are only able to effectively manage a total of 150 relationships.

This restriction is not just about brain capacity; it has implications for our ability to connect meaningfully in general. Although we can easily keep up with the lives and interests of thousands, this is an investment of our time. Investing time in superficial relationships online comes at the expense of investing time into meaningful ones. Over time, we accidentally erode our meaningful relationships which further impacts our ability to connect.

As we saw in the previous chapter, we now have the technology and tools, but how can we utilize these new tools for good? Saud has made it his mission to do just that. As he outlined when we spoke, he feels that it is vital that he becomes part of the solution rather than feeding into the growing problem of isolation and loneliness driven by click-bait social media – a problem that has driven youth suicide rates to increase by 56 per cent in the last decade in the United States alone.[27] After speaking with other friends who went through the same experience, Saud launched Picnic Ventures in 2019, a social media platform with social health at its core. Based on the premise of close and meaningful conversations, Picnic aims to save the social media landscape as we know it. As Saud puts it: 'Current social media networks are like eating fast food all the time. Sure, it's delicious and keeps you coming back for more, but sooner or later you are going to get sick.'

> ### THREE CORE VALUES
>
> We have now explored the three core values that are fundamental in the future of work:
>
> 1 positive change;
>
> 2 work–life balance;
>
> 3 meaningful connections.

Values must remain core or you will lose

As we have seen with the sudden launch of sharing economy apps, we are beginning to see businesses that promote these key values emerge as front-runners. Conversely, many antecedent unicorns who have shifted their original focus from doing good to doing well have begun to fall at the last fence.

Uber is one such antecedent unicorn. Initially launched as a business where doing good was at its core – the concept being that people didn't have to work in jobs they hated just to pay the bills. Uber promoted the idea that people could do what they loved (artist, musician, baker) and supplement their income with their car. Fast forward to 2020 and it is clear they have strayed far from their idealistic beginnings.

When Uber launched in 2009 their driver fees were low and incentives were high. Reports of how Uber would change the world as we knew it were prevalent. But by 2017 a report claiming that only 4 per cent of all Uber drivers were still working as such one year after entering the company showed how far they had drifted.[28] It seems that once they gained market share, the collaborative peer-to-peer environment with the idealistic goal of 'wealth on the side in your own time' soon led to driver fees upwards of 60 per cent of the fare. By 2019 drivers were earning $3.75 per hour after expenses.[29] Uber drivers are now working longer hours in order to pay rent, often working shifts that endanger themselves and others, a far cry from the original mission to help the artist in need.

Throughout this shift in Uber's market capitalization has been a corporate image marred by scandals involving data abuse, misleading drivers, gender discrimination, intellectual property theft and sexual assault or abuse of passengers. Despite it all, Uber still managed to raise $25 billion before their initial public offering on 9 May 2019, an IPO that was openly called a 'train wreck' by widely followed technology analyst Roger McNamee. Following the bell ringing, Uber managed a market capitalization at just $69 billion, significantly below the valuation of $120 billion that was pitched the previous year. Their devaluation was caused by their image. As McNamee puts it:

> There are two underlying assumptions in this business, both of which, in my mind, are questionable. One is that there is an unlimited supply of people with cars who are willing to drive for an amount of money that is, in many cities, below the minimum wage. And that, secondly, there will never be any blowback from cities and from drivers for the behaviour of this company. And I think both of those assumptions are not sound.[30]

It is the call out on the consequences of the business's behaviour which is particularly relevant and sadly not atypical.

The quick rise and fall due to ethics and morals has become a recurrent theme among Silicon Valley start-ups. Many, much like Uber, started off with lofty goals of doing good, but quickly shifted gears to profitability, eroding trust among customers and employees alike.

Another tech unicorn which has fallen dramatically is WeWork. Upon filing their IPO paperwork on 14 August 2019, WeWork publicly spiralled out of control following scrutiny of their finances and leadership, moving from their $47 billion valuation to just $2.9 billion after Softbank took over and removed Adam Neumann as CEO.[31] Their IPO is delayed indefinitely.

The values of work–life balance and connectivity were what launched these technology companies. They aimed to help people leverage their personal resources and make better use of excess capacity. The upside is that these businesses have shaped the world as we know it and increased competitive pressure on legacy services to adapt or die. However, their shift from aspiring to do good to their relentless drive to do well has become part of their downfall.

New businesses are taking note and the value of doing good is no longer just whitewash but mandatory to avoid the car crash of inflated unicorn valuations and failed IPOs that have come before. In the future of work, only businesses that are built with the golden trinity of values (positive change, work–life balance and meaningful connections) will achieve unicorn status.

A business that understands this is BrewDog. When they needed to raise finance they went to their customers, not their bank. Launching Equity for Punks which sells equity stakes in their company via the website, BrewDog has raised tens of millions in several equity crowdfunding rounds since 2009. In a time when small business financing is abysmal, looking to your network may be the only way. Therefore, learning how to communicate and connect to that network becomes paramount to success in the future of work. And this way of working collaboratively pays off. Following a recent private equity company acquiring 22 per cent of the company, the original Equity for Punks crowdfunders were able to sell a portion of their stock, making a 2,765 per cent return on their initial investment.[32] Not bad for a couple of punks.

CHAPTER FIVE

Earning the right to lead

Are leaders born or bred?

On 24 September 2018 at 3.47 am I lay awake staring at the ceiling of my hotel room at White City House in London, England. It was dark, but the glow from the old BBC Studios down below illuminated my room just enough to make out the details on the chandelier that hung above my bed. I had landed 15 hours earlier on the red eye from Los Angeles. I had not slept for 32 hours. And yet despite trying everything I could think of I could not get myself to sleep.

Maybe it was the jetlag. Maybe it was nerves.

I knew I needed to get some rest before what would be a very big day. A big day that started at 7 am; just three hours and 13 minutes to go before my alarm. I kept checking the clock. My first conference call was at 7.15 am with my website designer. It was well before the time their digital agency opened, but he was jumping on the call at my demand to have my new website up and running before 9 that morning. I had noticed several errors on the red eye and had sent him the list before my plane touched down at Heathrow Airport. It was a long list.

As the clock ticked onwards and my hand grew weary from hitting repeat on the sleep app I was unsuccessfully using at the time, I finally gave up at 4.53 am, got out of bed and took a shower. I figured I might as well work rather than just lie there all night thinking of everything that could go wrong that morning. I had a couple of hours until my web designer would be up and at his desk, so I paced the room and compiled to-do lists on the hotel letterhead I found in my nightstand.

I love nothing more than a to-do list. It is one of my favourite ways to pass the time, detailing all the things I need to get done. Despite having online platforms and apps that do this, I personally love putting pen to paper. It makes crossing off items feel that much more rewarding.

While I paced and wrote lists, I realized that this sleepless night was the first time I had ever worked through the night. I work hard, like anyone else, but I have always been speedy. I have also never been so detail oriented that things not done perfectly keep me up at night, which I know can be a qualm for some perfectionists. But this was slightly different. With a press announcement coming out in the morning and scheduled communications announcing my next venture – the first since selling my agency – I wanted to ensure that everything was perfect and my website was the cornerstone to this.

Unlike many who consider their website an afterthought, I believe a website is core to your business. It is the first impression you give to compel anyone searching through the online high street to buy your wares. And like the physical retail outlets, your storefront window is critical. No one knows this more than luxury London retailer Harrods which spends millions on its window displays. Even real estate agents know the trick to selling a house for 17 per cent more than the recommended listing price comes down to how you stage that house.[1] And yet these lessons rarely cross over into the online world. Still so few spend the time or the money ensuring their website says exactly what they want it to.

Over the years I have discovered that there is an adeptness to creating a good website. This was what was keeping me up that night. Knowing that if I was going to take a leap out of my comfort zone into the unknown a second time, the least I could do was ensure that my website was above reproach.

It all began after I sold my first business in 2016. Following the sale, I decided to take a year off from working. Instead, I'd fill my time by saying 'yes'. I called it my Year of Yes. This saw me do the things I'd always wanted to, but never had the time while I grew my business. Some things were basic, like being a dog walker for my neighbour and going to the dentist. Others were monumental like getting married. And some were just for fun such as going to the Burning Man festival in Nevada and wine tasting in Napa Valley. I also took part in a popular reality TV show. It was a busy year.

But I promised myself that after my Year of Yes, I would get back to work. Having spent my career to date selling intangible sponsorship opportunities, I wanted to try my hand at some-thing tangible. Something that you could touch, taste and see. A product that you could sell with properties rather than hopes and dreams. I landed on wine. Because honestly, why not? More specifically ice wine, a speciality from my hometown in Canada.

Ice wine is made by leaving grapes on the vine past harvest until they freeze naturally below −8C. They are handpicked, often at 4 am when it is the coldest outside. These hard frozen marbles are then pressed into juice that goes through the typical wine fermenting process to create a luxury sweet wine. Almost unheard of outside of North America, Germany and China, I wanted to take this 200-year-old process and reinvent it for the younger generation. It aimed to be a disruptor in a stagnant market. I had a clear vision of how I wanted to communicate this luxury, maverick brand – and it was all riding on this one website which a press release would soon direct the world to. The website that was keeping me awake.

In hindsight this was probably not something I should have stressed about; I had been in much stickier work-related situations before, but nonetheless I felt the pressure. The wording needed to be exact, the imagery perfect. I poured over sentences a hundred times, rearranging the words and the font sizes until I thought it looked faultless. Because this was a new product launching in a cluttered market, I needed to find the right tone of voice that provided both education and an edge. The tagline on the homepage, 'Be Different', evolved through a thousand variations until I felt it went in the direction in which I wanted the product to go.

By the time my web designer Tom called, I had a million things I needed him to change, all before 9 am when the press release went out. If he was stressed, he did not let on.

At 8.58 am the website went live. The press release went out at 9.00 am and by 9.01 am I was officially in business with my new company REBEL Pi Ice Wine. It was a niche product and at the luxury price point of US $169/bottle, also for a niche audience. I had not worked in wine before this, a small detail that would not deter me. As I learned earlier with my first business, I knew success can be achieved with minimal experience as long as you take the time to learn along the way.

It took me three months to gain traction in the wine trade. Longer than I had expected. Some simple things I had not accounted for, such as discovering restaurants purchase wine from distributors rather than direct, and others I plain overlooked. In hindsight much of it was common sense, but it created a setback on sales. But by the time January came around I had built my own community within the wine industry. By February I was asked to judge wine events, and by March I was on the speaking circuit and had a wine column in a popular trade magazine. My REBEL Pi Ice Wine itself even won a few prestigious awards. As my personal profile in the wine industry grew, my product became a cult favourite and was listed at some of the best Michelin star restaurants in London.

By creating my own wine brand, I knew I would gain new experience in development, branding and product sales. What I did not expect to learn was how similar some of my leadership experiences would be in wine to those of my first business in sponsorship – two completely different businesses in everything from set-up, to execution and profitability. Where my sponsorship agency had four global offices in which I managed teams of up to 50 people in multiple languages, my wine business was run from a tiny desk in the corner of my bedroom. Where I spent thousands of dollars entertaining prospective clients to generate sales in my first business, my ice wine bottles could be gifted to entice large retail buyers. The two businesses could not have been more different. And yet, my quick rise as a leader in both was almost identical.

Because the two industries did not have any crossover of people working within them, the similarities became more apparent as time went on. The wine trade knew little of my previous entrepreneurial journey and the sponsorship industry barely registered that I owned a wine brand. Yet both continued to utilize me for content creation (podcasts, interviews, articles, blogs) and events (speaking, panels, organizing committees). I managed to earn leadership across both industries within months of launching and without any experience in either.

My ability to do this twice in two disparate industries with contrasting business models proves my actions were not a coincidence. Rather, it confirms that basic methods and processes can be put in place to ensure you can cultivate leadership.

Defining leadership

At this point it is important to note that leadership is not influence, although influence can play a role in identifying a leader. Where influence is the ability to make people take action

– most often purchase something – true leadership is about inspiring a network towards collective thought that leads to collective action. We have discussed leadership throughout this book in terms of achieving greatness beyond the boundaries of what has historically been possible. The potential to lead the world into doing good, not just doing well. Leadership that can take the new technological tools that have been developed to shift us into a better way of working. A way of working that is conducive to progress, growth and well-being. A way of working that aligns with our personal belief systems and not necessarily one that lines our bank accounts. True leadership to inspire future generations. We are no longer cemented in the world that has been created for us; instead we can define our future by breaking old rules and evolving the future of work as we know it.

As the world becomes smaller and more accessible, the importance of understanding how to collaborate and connect vast networks is critical. To do so requires a new set of skills. It requires new leadership to manage this opportunity in a positive way. New leadership to start a movement, whether that is on a global stage, within the confines of your business, or within your own community. The potential for change is now possible, and rebellious leadership is the access point to making that change happen.

Leadership is defined by standing up for what you believe in and inspiring others to do the same. Thought leadership is just one component of new leadership, but it also creates the foundation for earned leadership. Without a strong concept of what you believe in and leading the change through authentic and genuine communications, you will never be able to assemble and inspire the network you want. Thought leadership is launched by developing a strong sense of self and having the confidence to put that into action. Only then can true rebellious leadership have the integrity needed to inspire the rest of the world.

Inspiration is integral to the future of work. Without the promise of pension funds and the stability of corporate culture, inspiration is now the only tool to move people into action. This sounds more challenging than it is. In truth, inspiration is already the source for everything we do. We just need to apply it within the constructs of the future of work.

We have spent the first part of this book outlining the history of business and how digital technologies and the internet have reshaped everything we thought we knew about leadership and work. We now need to look at the practical steps to becoming a leader in this new, and ever radically evolving, world we find ourselves in. What do we need to do to take advantage of this change and how do we do so quickly? As we have seen in the previous pages, we no longer have the luxury of time, so let us start by exploring the fundamentals required for everyone to take advantage. The goal is to capitalize on this shift by altering our mindset and focussing on what matters most, rather than being paralysed into inaction while others adapt.

My aim is to prove that everyone has the potential to become a new leader in the future of work by breaking some rules and tapping into their rebelliousness. My promise is that by becoming a rebel leader you will unlock your personal success pathway defined by new rules. Finally, it is my hope that this book inspires you into action because I believe real change is possible. It just requires all of us to participate.

Ultimately, I want you to become a leader who stands for something and aims to make positive change – whether that is leading your community, your business or even your household. But before we begin to lead, we must earn it.

New rules to earn leadership

Rule One: Find your passion

OLD RULE = FOLLOW THE MONEY

NEW RULE = FOLLOW YOUR PASSION

By this point in the book it should be abundantly clear that being purpose-driven and purposeful in work are essential in today's changing environment. It is now crucial to look at how one becomes purposeful. To be clear, being purposeful in the future of work does not necessarily mean you need to have a business that is purpose-driven – for example running a non-profit organization. You can still run a for-profit company and lead with purpose. You can also have a business that has a strong purpose and not be personally aligned to that purpose. The two things are not correlational. The trick is ensuring your personal purpose is aligned.

This is no mean feat.

The task is challenging because we are constrained by the shackles of our history, our education and our experiences. If everything we ever learned about business is now redundant it makes for a very difficult journey to discover the right path that works for us.

The reason we rely on history and experience is because they provide a short cut for us to make decisions. However, as we have argued throughout this book, the short cuts that have worked in the past no longer give us the right information to base our decisions on in the future. Most of us are making decisions relying on the wrong information. To start making decisions with the right information, we need to work much harder to sift through the constant onslaught of information while being steadfast in our own truth. Not everyone has the time, the energy or the capacity to do this. And that is perfectly fine. However, for you to achieve unbounded success in the future of work, I argue that this is absolutely fundamental, and it becomes the first step to achieving success as a rebellious leader.

In school we are asked what we aspire to be, but never what we care about most. If you recall earlier I shared that as a child I wanted to work at the local ice cream shop so I feel this is a fairly arbitrary assessment. In business school we utilize historical case studies to understand basic business practices, accounting principles and management tactics. Our entire education provides examples – paths paved by others. Extraordinarily little time is spent looking inward and taking the time to discover what it is we are most passionate about. But it is this passion, this internal drive, that will give you the grit required to gather the right information to allow you to make the right decisions for yourself. This will ultimately lead to your success in the future of work.

The concept of grit as a predictor of success is especially topical following Angela Duckworth's viral TED Talk, which has generated over 19 million views since it was uploaded in 2013, and bestselling book *Grit: The power of passion and perseverance*. As Duckworth defines it: 'Grit is passion and sustained persistence applied towards long-term achievement, with no particular concern for rewards or recognition along the way.' Specifically to matters of success, she outlines that 'talent and luck matter to success... grit may matter at least as much, if not more.'[2]

Grit has also been acknowledged as a reason that underdogs win. Malcolm Gladwell, author of bestseller *David and Goliath*, further explored this theory, focussing on the probability of improbable events. Specifically, he investigated stories where the underdog beats the odds. Through his research he discovered the shocking fact that Goliath wins only 66 per cent of the time.[3] This is barely more predictive than a coin toss. And yet our strong assumptions, built through a history of storytelling passed down through generations, means we expect Goliath to win every time.

This is not atypical. Our world is built on storytelling. Stories which have not been fact checked for centuries. Understandably as our world has evolved, so too have many of the outcomes of these folklores.

This begs the question: Is what we think true, indeed true?

Gladwell goes on to explain that underdogs are more successful in real life than in storytelling because they refuse to compete by the same standards as their opponents. Instead they rely on entirely different strategies that exploit their stronger opponent's weaknesses. So, winning as an underdog is more common in life than stories, experience and education lead us to believe. This fact dispels the general assumption that we should want to be Goliath if we want to be a winner.

This is particularly relevant to what we are exploring as it further exemplifies how rebel leaders are winning more than they are losing. It also hints that rebels are potentially not the rebels we have been brought up to chastise, but rather the leaders we want to emulate.

Outliers are no longer outliers. If Gladwell updated his research, I suspect that a pattern would emerge where the Davids of this world start overtaking Goliaths more frequently than just 34 per cent.

And if grit provides the starting point to becoming a more successful David, how does one accumulate more grit? While Duckworth outlines several clever ways to grow it, I think it can easily be summed up by 'passion'. Understanding what personally motivates you and what your values are is the easiest starting point to ensure a grittier outcome towards your success.

Too many times in interviews I am asked the same question: 'What drives or motivates you?' I find this irritating. The underlying assumption is that there must be something greater than what I do to drive me to work as hard as I do, to achieve the success I have achieved. The underlying postulation being that my work could not possibly be enough to give me the grit I have shown throughout my business journey so far. However, it is not the right question to ask because what has driven me are the businesses themselves. I am truly passionate about what I am doing because it aligns with my values, regardless of whether that work is in sponsorship, wine or technology. It is my personal passion which gets me out of bed in the morning. Without it, I lack the inspiration to do much more beyond watching the *Real Housewives of Beverly Hills* all day in loungewear.

If you are finding yourself stuck in a rut with little motivation to move forward, the best first step is to start at the beginning. We have all been in situations where decisions are made and we end up in a place we never expected, or we expected would make us happy, but didn't. There is no shame in not living a fulfilled life. It is your life. However, if you want to be more fulfilled and inspired to lead, then you must go back to basics.

When I am inspired and my values align to the work I am doing, you cannot stop me. It is that alignment to my fundamental values that keeps me from being a couch potato or endlessly scrolling Instagram. I am truly passionate about the things that I say I am passionate about. When I set up my first sponsorship business, I wanted to prove that my thinking on creating commercially profitable partnerships beyond badging and logos was correct. I was passionate about proving others wrong. I was passionate about showing people I could do it. In simple terms, I was passionate about being right. With my second business, ice wine allowed me to be creative and learn about an industry I knew nothing about. I found the people and the businesses fascinating and this drove me to learn more about what I was doing and evolve my strategy.

It is passion that gets me out of bed each morning. It is passion that gives me the grit I need to persevere for the long term and pave my own path. As we are all different, everyone's passion points will be different, but the first step is to find out what it is that you are most passionate about. Only then will you be able to unlock the grit required to succeed as a leader.

Once you are passionate about something and communicate that passion to the world, you no longer have to drag your employees or your community along with you on your journey. Instead, your passion alone will be the inspiration needed to gain followers who support you. They stop working for you and instead begin to work *with* you because your passion ignites their passion. In the future of work there is no leadership without passion, but it is what that passion does for others that is critical. Passion inspires people and it is that inspiration that is necessary to be a successful leader. By aligning yourself to others with similar passions and igniting their drive through inspiration you too can achieve greatness.

But, first things first, we must identify our personal passions today if we are to become the leaders of tomorrow.

Here are my steps to discovering your personal passion:

A **Write down your values:** Think about the top five things you care about and put pen to paper. Being passionate does not necessarily mean saving the world. If you value money, then there is no shame in that. It is more important to write down the things you actually value, rather than what you think you should value or what your friends value. A trick is also to look at who you find inspirational and why. By understanding other people's values and how they inspire you, you begin to be able to look inward.

B **Write down the activities you love to do:** What makes you happiest? Is it being with your family, or getting loose on the dancefloor? Start to analyse your activities daily and identify the things you do because you love to do them versus things you do because you must do them.

C **Figure out what you are good at:** This is important because people tend to like things more when they are good at them. Liking what you do is important for igniting your passion in work and in leadership. For example, despite running several different teams, I am not great at managing people. Not being great at something is soul-destroying for me and so understandably managing people is something I dread. I am, however, particularly good at getting everyone together and having fun. And I like doing that. Over the years I have managed to make this work for me. In business, I no longer bother with management meetings or staff reviews; instead I spend quality time with employees at the pub. This works for me because it is what I am better at doing. It works for them because most people do not like to pass up free drinks and time out of the office. But fundamentally I am a better leader because I am not forcing actions or activities that I am both terrible at and do not enjoy doing into my daily work life which would negatively impact my team. The outcome of understanding where my staff are, if they are happy and whether they like their job, is the same; however, the execution is quite different. By having an execution that aligns to my passion, it becomes more enjoyable for everyone involved. The more enjoyable, the more effective.

D **Go out and test your thinking:** Writing things down on a piece of paper is helpful to consolidate your thoughts and provides a starting point; however, as my mother always says: 'Actions speak louder than words.' Do not be afraid to test yourself. If you put sustainability as a key value you hold dear but are rarely seen putting anything in the recycling bin then you need to question whether the values you think you hold most dear are really the values you care about. Be honest.

E **Prioritize:** You cannot value a hundred things equally, so pick your top five and put them in order. This will not only help with growing your grit in the future, it will help with starting you off on the right foot – you want to find something that aligns to your number one value and ideally supports other values below. It does not work if you set off with a purpose based on a value you only partially care about. This is very much an all or nothing exercise for it to work and be effective.

A lot of people, including myself, read business books for a bit of inspiration and a bit of know-how, but when it comes to recommendations and practical implementation, we rarely put in the work. But if there is one thing that I would strongly recommend doing in this book it is taking time to think about what it is that you really love to do. Without this, you will never truly reach your potential – rebel leader or not. High-achieving success and leadership do not happen without a significant amount of strife and effort, but without passion, you have nothing to fall back on when the challenges get tough. For this reason alone, it is critical to be clear with yourself about what really motivates and drives you.

Rule Two: Gain confidence to stand up for what you believe in

OLD RULE = DON'T ROCK THE BOAT

NEW RULE = STAND FOR SOMETHING

Identifying your passion will help drive you, but it is unlikely to drive people to you unless you are able to communicate your passion to the world. This book is not about fulfilment (although it is likely one of the many outcomes), but about leadership, and leadership is not about achieving personal success. Leadership is the action of inspiring a group of people towards achieving a common goal. While passion will provide you with your own personal happiness and fulfilment in the work that you choose to do, communication is the critical lynchpin that progresses it from an individual pursuit into a mass movement.

Many people struggle with this step for a variety of reasons. Current leaders shy away from taking a stance because they are too afraid their viewpoints may not match those of their prospective clients or customers. They choose to be generic in order to appease everyone rather than stand by their values and lose potential market share. External communications from leaders and organizations that take this viewpoint are often vague. Their corporate mission statements are written so they could mean anything to anyone, and that is precisely the point. But because visibility is so much greater today, that no longer works as a strategy. Now more than ever it is not just clients or customers that leaders need to be aligned with; it is also employees. While historically leaders focussed on the bottom line, aligning values is now crucial. As we have outlined with Amazon employee walkouts for climate change, it is now important for leaders to stand *for* something.

We need leaders to be clear about what it is they stand for. We need businesses to be transparent in how they execute their mission statements. What a business does and what a leader says are key to how individuals choose to live their lives. There is an interconnectedness between work and life, whether you are working for a business or purchasing a product. The choices we make are now influential.

Compounding the issue is that a leader's values need to be clear enough to cut through the noise. As we are bombarded with up to 10,000 advertisements each day, almost all unsolicited, our brains need to be selective in the information we retain and engage with.[4] Often the clearer the message, the easier it is for our brains to digest.

As outlined in Chapter 4, the information we often choose to assimilate is that which aligns with our values or that which is provided by someone who mirrors ourselves. Vague information that creates confusion is quickly disregarded. Therefore, for your organization, your brand or yourself to stand out you need something to stand for, otherwise you will be lost in the ether of information overload.

It may seem that only bold brands and personalities like BrewDog can capitalize on confidently standing for what they believe in as a means towards success, because bold messages (and in BrewDog's specific case bold press stunts) have a greater ability to cut through the media. However, it is very important to clarify that you do not need to be a rebel, a pirate or a punk to become a rebellious leader. When we refer to rebellious leadership we are referencing the ability and desire to challenge concepts and restrictions long held in business. To consider alternatives and not be restrained in thought or potential. To ask 'Why not?' more often, rather than succumb to the status quo. You do not need to be a tattoo adorned, out-spoken, loudmouth to be successful as a rebellious leader, as activist Greta Thunberg has proven.

Born on 3 January 2003, Thunberg is slight for her age at 5 ft tall. She likes to wear Velcro sneakers and wears her sandy-coloured hair in braided pigtails parted down the middle. She is soft-spoken and loves horses. She is, on the face of it, a very typical teenager. However, this teenager is anything but typical. At just 16 years of age, Thunberg was chosen as *Time*'s Person of the Year in 2019 for her efforts in addressing the climate crisis, a title which she shares with a roster of significant global leaders including Martin Luther King Jr, Mahatma Gandhi, Jimmy Carter and Jeff Bezos.[5]

Unbelievably, her activism started only a year earlier in August 2018 when she did something most typical teenagers do, skipped school. But rather than going to the shopping mall, Thunberg took a cardboard sign painted in black letters that read *Skolstrejk för klimatet*: School Strike for Climate. On the cold stone steps of the Swedish Parliament she would sit with homemade paper flyers in black ink that read: 'My name is Greta, I am in ninth grade, and I am school-striking for the climate. Since you adults don't give a damn about my future, I won't either.'[6] It was the simplicity of that statement that launched an avalanche of a movement. By the end of 2018 tens of thousands of students across Europe began skipping school to protest alongside her. By September 2019 it was estimated 4 million people showed up to protest, including 250,000 who marched in New York City and 100,000 in London. In just over a year Thunberg inspired the world through the simple act of skipping school.

Thunberg personifies the point that leadership is not about how loud you shout, but how strongly you stand. As an individual Thunberg is the opposite of what one would typically expect as a rebel, and yet she personifies rebellious leadership, with people from every country identifying with her and standing in solidarity beside her. Where many others have failed to bring attention to the climate crisis, Thunberg and her cardboard sign succeeded in creating a global shift with real parliamentary-level change. She inspired the world to act. Specifically, she managed the incredible feat of inspiring the entire world to act towards her vision and her values, all by having the confidence to communicate what it is she stands for. Just three little words hand-painted on a homemade cardboard sign in a small country.

It is important to remember that change does not have to be astronomical to be effective. Think back to David Brailsford's marginal gains theory. Small changes over time can produce significant results. From a communications perspective you can apply this by regularly communicating your passion in small ways that can contribute to a greater change overall. You just need to know what it is you stand for and have the confidence in yourself to stand up for it.

Having the confidence to stand up for what you believe in is a consistent trait among new leaders in the future of work, as we will discover in the coming chapters. It is this active communication against the status quo which has historically characterized them as pirates, rebels and disrupters; however, it is more commonplace simply because online communications provide a greater platform to amplify their message. It is the power of these new voices gained through their ability to confidently stand up for what they believe in which is revolutionary and necessary for positive change to happen.

Rule Three: Use clear and consistent messaging

OLD RULE = FAKE IT TILL YOU MAKE IT

NEW RULE = BE AUTHENTIC

Thunberg is also a good example of positive change through the power of communication whose straightforward speaking manner is often cited as one of the reasons her messages gained traction so quickly. This straightforward manner is often cited is a symptom of having Asperger's, a developmental disorder characterized by significant difficulties in social interaction and nonverbal communication.[7] A disorder that she acknowledges makes her different. As she puts it: 'Given the right circumstances – being different is a superpower.'[8]

In a world where we aim to fit in, this viewpoint is refreshing. Not only is it OK to be different, it is a benefit.

Thunberg's simple message catapulted her onto the global stage, acquiring a loyal following along the way. Clear statements such as 'I am in ninth grade, and I am school-striking for the climate' enabled others to immediately understand what her values were and what she stood for. Her flyers did not include a call to action, the holy grail of direct marketing, but instead left it to the reader to decide for themselves what action, if any, to take. Rather than ask people to join forces, it is much simpler for people to join of their own volition. It is also much more effective.

According to psychologist Albert Bandura, observing other people's actions can prompt the viewer to engage in behaviour already learned.[9] His theory argues that behaviours and actions are not elicited in isolated instances to understand consequences or results. Instead humans observe others and then make their own choices, usually decisions made from information they had gathered previously. These choices then become part of their self-efficacy system, emphasizing the role in determining and developing their personality. This is directly linked to the ability to achieve goals.

In the case of clear and consistent messaging this is paramount. People need to be given clear choices along their journey and your messaging is one such choice, to align or not align with you. If you are unclear about what you stand for, it becomes impossible to make a choice. This is often the hurdle when movements fail to gain the traction they should. For example, the climate crisis is not a new concern; however, historically the threat was confused by scientific facts and figures which made it hard for people to jump on board with their support. It took simple wording repeated in straightforward language for a movement to begin.

Simplicity and consistency are critical. Your messaging must be consistent across all your communication channels, actions and output – whether that is your business model, your Twitter feed, or simply aligning the reasons you chose to skip school. Inconsistent messaging will not gain momentum because it is unclear to the listener what behaviour you are eliciting and what values you deem important, making those actions impossible to mirror for themselves.

Following Thunberg's lead, if the messaging is simple and consistent you will gain followers who not only display the same behaviour but also have the same desire to communicate the message. As a result, the skewed viewpoint of mass media is being replaced by organic and authentic individual communications of many who are all aligned.

We are exposed to so much more now. So, like the media networks and television studios that went before, it is now important for us to strategically consider how our personal communications contribute to shaping the world around us. What we put on social media affects others, influencing behaviours through modelling. We are now part of the system.

This new shift in communication power works in two ways. If your desired outcome (ie gaining a following of advocates) is not working as effectively as you had planned, then you need to review your communications. Are they consistent? Would people identify you through your content without knowing your name or your company's brand?

If you are not gaining the traction you hoped for, it is likely due to mismanagement of your communications. Although we recognize this immediately when it relates to social media ads and product placement with influencers, this effect also comes into play with your personal communications. If your feed includes what you ate for breakfast, your love of cycling, motivating tips for doing bicep curls and a picture of your cat Kevin, there is no clear message for the viewer. Without a clear message it makes it incredibly challenging for people to align with. And we already know people are busy. We need to make things easy. If you want to be a leader in your field, you must be single-goal-oriented in your communications. This is not to say you cannot love your cat Kevin, just keep him out of your newsfeed.

On the other hand, if you happen to post bikini-clad images from your recent sun-soaked holiday and saw your online following skyrocket but are trying to make a name for yourself as a keynote speaker in human resource management then you are missing the point of growing a network. Having millions of people follow you for one reason (sexy bikini images) will not provide you with the platform for what it is you really want to stand for (as a thought leader). This is not to say you cannot be a sexy bikini model *and* a computer programmer, as fashion model Karlie Kloss has proven, but people who want to see posts on both subjects are few. As Bandura discovered, if you want to create change through your actions, you need people to identify with your values for them to be able to mimic those same actions. The value must be obvious or else the message will be lost.

The expectation that growing followers for one thing will allow you to later transition them to something else you care about does not work for most people, unless you are a Kardashian. To become a true leader, one that inspires a movement, you need your actions and communications to be replicated. Having lots of followers for no reason other than seeing your Instagram likes increase is not a method of building true leadership.

Once you create clear and consistent messaging around the values you hold, you then need to remain unwavering in the execution of your communications. Expect that when you have an opinion not everyone will agree with your perspective. That is OK. Social media is a hotbed for online trolls who would never say anything to your face but enjoy picking people apart from the safety of their laptop. It is important to remember this is the format of the platform and not a personal slight against you. You must not let online rejection discourage you. Too often criticism makes people second-guess their decisions and choices, typically decisions and choices they have already thought long and hard about. Taking in information is certainly important when it comes to making choices, but critiques from strangers should not be enough to stop you from saying what you truly think. Personally, I just imagine all online trolls are living in their parents' garage and spend most of the day in their underwear. Not exactly the type of people I would listen to.

BEING ON BRAND IS NOT JUST FOR BRANDS

It is worth mentioning that being unwavering is critical to remaining on brand. It is this consistency despite criticism that proves your determination to the cause at hand. Going back to Duckworth's theory on grit, 'sustained persistence' is crucial to your success. Your goals and personal aims now become highly visible because of social media. Your actions, and subsequent reactions, must support your messaging because your messaging is the output of your values.

No one knows the value of being 'on brand' more than Lauryn Evarts Bosstick. As the founder and lifestyle blogger behind *The Skinny Confidential*, Bosstick may look like your everyday influencer, but she has utilized communications so effectively that she has become a brand herself. An entrepreneur at her core, her determined tenacity to build on what started as a health and fitness blog has seen her launch a book, a podcast with over 54 million listens (featuring everyone from Jessica Alba to Molly Sims) and an online following that reaches millions. She is one of the few to successfully bridge the gap between content creator and entrepreneur.

A quick scan of Bosstick's Instagram and you can tell she likes pink. A further view of her content and you realize her irritating lack of capitals in her sentences is a clever branding tactic. Beyond some of these visual tricks, her irreverent language creates a juxtaposition with the topics she discusses. Content that focusses on helping her community be their best selves – from being more efficient to coping with a bad boss. This career-focussed content is then mixed in with beauty recommendations, ensuring she does not stray too far from the community which initially built her up. Regardless of what she posts or talks about, it is clear she values sharing tips, with the aim that her followers 'become the best version of themselves'.[10] In this day and age where being ourselves is now more paramount to our life path, who does not want that?

Living in Los Angeles, Bosstick is every bit the LA blonde bombshell you would expect to find talking health and wellness. Her can-do attitude projects into your headphones with every podcast episode you listen to. It makes you consider whether you should be drinking the same juice she mixes every morning. But when it comes to execution, she is relentless. As she puts it: 'At my core, I'm a writer. I'm a creative… I really respect my audience's time.'[11]

Her effortless transition from content creator to podcaster has been made with strategic insight and planning. Launching her podcast was not an attempt to get on the bandwagon but because she believes audio is the future of content. She wants to be one of the first. Bosstick is a prime example of how being consistent with messaging to remain on brand, regardless of the medium or platform, provides space for pivoting into other areas of interest. Her quick rise proves consistency and authenticity work.

Rule Four: Be knowledgeable

OLD RULE = HIRE AN EXPERT

NEW RULE = BE THE EXPERT

As Stewart Brand dreamed, we now have the tools to help us make better decisions. The internet has given us the means to learn about anything for free. From discussing rock formations in the Andes to becoming a doula, if you can dream it, you can do it. There are no excuses for not educating yourself in the area you wish to lead. Being knowledgeable supports having an opinion. Being knowledgeable is your armour to gain followers.

To clarify, this is not to say you need a doctorate on the subject you care about, but it does mean your interest should propel your curiosity. You should be aware of the arguments for and against what you stand for, be eager to discuss them, and be interested to push the conversation forward.

Not only has the internet provided direct access to information, it has also given direct access to people. Whether that is actively utilized in peer-to-peer discussions in online forums, or by passively listening to podcasts and reading blogs – our ability to tap into resources is unlimited. This needs to be used to your advantage to earn leadership. As they say, 'knowledge is power'.

Like the rules outlined, this too is easier said than done. With so much information out there, staying on top of it all can be daunting. For example, if 'family' is your biggest value then you could spend a lifetime digesting all the information online related to successfully raising a family. And do not even get started on video content. YouTube alone sees an average of 18,000 days' worth of videos uploaded daily.[12]

Regardless of the mountain of data that you will never fully be able to assimilate, it is still vital to utilize as much information available to gain credibility through knowledge. Rather than encroaching on your circadian rhythms with middle-of-the-night online searches, your ability to access knowledge can be strategically implemented and habit-forming. The aim is to make the overwhelming task of staying on top of information much easier to integrate into your already busy life.

Here are my methods to ensure I stay top of my game in whatever field I am working in:

A **Google alerts/social media notifications tools**: Use the internet wisely. There are several online tools that allow you to push information into your inbox or your social media feed on an hourly, daily or monthly basis. These tools are incredibly easy to set up and can be managed as your journey evolves. If your search term is too wide and your inbox is inundated with junk, then refine the terms until you get exactly what you are looking for, with a volume of content that you can realistically digest. Not only does this save you time searching for articles that are interesting and relatable, it also structures your day so that you receive all the new information on your chosen topic in one shot, known as task batching – which in itself is incredibly effective and highly recommended.

Task batching is a time management system that maximizes concentration, productivity, creativity and mental clarity by grouping similar tasks together. By batching sourced information into your inbox at one time with Google Alerts rather than searching when the moment strikes you, you are able to cut down the time it takes for your brain to switch activities and refocus. This process is comparable to the productivity of the supply chains in manufacturing. Just as changing lines in a supply chain cuts into margins and kills profitability, so too does constantly changing direction in your mind. By incorporating long periods of focussed concentration, be that in reading information or executing an action, you can be more productive. As we are constantly incorporating more into our daily lives, our time to focus on learning and gaining knowledge is typically the one task that most people do not prioritize. By batching your information and knowledge through online tools you can ensure continued learning remains a constant priority in your schedule.

B **Engage:** Being a leader is more than just passively reading content. To be an effective leader, you must engage with that content. Engaging in online content is the active form of reading. Engaging includes commenting on articles, posts and topics by providing your viewpoint or questioning the writer's angle. Posting your opinion online will also sense-check your own opinion: 'Is this really what I think?'

This is not an easy first step, mostly because many people are embarrassed to ask questions and fear that their online comments will not resonate with the writer or other readers. Once you overcome your fear and make it a constant action against the information you read, it will become more natural and you will begin to curate your own tone of voice. The benefit is that over time your engagement will form the foundation of what you care about. It will inform how you communicate, while also ensuring you remain knowledgeable. Engaging also provides the added benefit of opening dialogue within your community, allowing you to connect with a greater number of people.

FEAR

If fear is holding you back from actively engaging both online and in person, I recommend going back to Rule Two in this chapter. These recommendations are building blocks, you cannot do one thing without fulfilling the previous step. Only once you break the old rules of the past and utilize all recommendations simultaneously will you then be able to tap into true rebellious leadership.

C **Listen:** Storytelling as a mechanism to disseminate knowledge has been around since the dawn of time. But as digital consumption increases, sadly our time to read decreases. In fact, the *The Washington Post* reported that since 2004 reading for pleasure has decreased a whopping 30 per cent.[13] With less spare time, people have a harder time picking up a book. But just because we are not picking up books does not mean we are not still sharing knowledge. Instead, we have turned to podcasts. As of January 2020, there were over 30 million episodes and over 900,000 podcast shows.[14] These shows are being listened to everywhere, by everyone, with 51 per cent of people reporting that they have listened to a podcast at least once.[15]

In addition to sharing knowledge, podcasting enables us to be informed in the fast-paced world we live in. Rather than wait for the publication of a business book in which many of the case studies outlined will be a year old before they hit the shelves, podcasting is in real time and reflects real-world situations. This is particularly important when it comes to health and safety. For example, within two months of the Covid-19 pandemic there were over 1,400 podcast episodes with titles including 'corona' or 'covid' and over 27.5 million downloads.[16] It is fast news, but on your time. We no longer need to rely on the evening news. So if you haven't already, start downloading podcasts to support you on your knowledge journey – a necessary component in the future of work.

EARN THE RIGHT TO LEAD

The four new rules of rebellious leadership:

    Rule One: Find your passion.

    Rule Two: Gain confidence.

    Rule Three: Use clear and consistent messaging.

    Rule Four: Be knowledgeable.

Now that leadership is granted by others, earning it becomes the new focus in the future of work. Old rules where leadership was confined to dark suits standing behind presidential podiums have been abolished. Instead we can find new leadership in the most unforeseen places – discovering that you can be a leader even if you wear Velcro shoes and skip school.

But new leadership is not granted easily. You must work hard at understanding yourself to lead with authenticity. Only then will you be able to tap into the inspiration necessary for others to follow.

Fortunately, as this chapter has outlined, everyone can become an enormously successful leader in the future of work by simply being a bit rebellious and breaking some old rules.

Now that we know which rules need to be broken, we need to ensure that old habits do not return. To that aim, we explore the importance of not becoming complacent – common among old leaders, but impossible to sustain in the future of work, as we will discover in the next chapter.

CHAPTER SIX

Complacency is not an option

Embracing failure during my 15 minutes of fame

Born in the 1980s, I have always been a fan of reality TV shows. The prominence of reality television was a component of my childhood and featured heavily in my teenage years. I liked to balance my hours spent watching *The Hills* with more 'culturally appropriate' episodes of *The Apprentice*. It was Donald Trump's series that got me hooked. The show was the perfect mix of hilarity and insight into career paths I might forge after graduation. I also loved the boardroom drama.

Those episodes replayed in my memory as I graduated and launched my career in my twenties. Throughout it all I continued to watch, compelled by the format. Like most people, I enjoyed watching with popcorn in hand while yelling 'What an idiot!' at the television screen. During those episodes I always fantasized about taking on *The Apprentice* tasks, but I never seriously thought about applying. I knew it was purely for entertainment. From over 30 seasons in both the United States and the United Kingdom, no one ever became much of a success following the 'You're Hired' final episode. This is understandable – no one wants to watch someone doing a good job on television; it does not grab headlines.

My longstanding relationship with the show changed one cold winter night in November 2017. I was lounging on my blue velvet sofa in London at the beginning of what would become my Year of Yes sabbatical watching reality television show reruns. Not the most ambitious way to start my year off, but my wonderful husband Chris had not yet quit his job to come galivanting around the world with me, so I found myself with a lot of spare time waiting to get going.

That night was no different, and yet it became the night that changed everything that year. It was right around the time *The Apprentice* started in the UK, prompting viewers to consider applying. Not something I would have normally taken notice of, but Lord Sugar caught my eye. Speaking directly to the camera in his pristine blue suit he outlined the ease of the application process and dangled the dream of becoming his business partner.

Having just sold my business where I owned 100 per cent of the company, being anyone's business partner at that point was quite off-putting, but I was intrigued by the process. Propelled by the pinot noir I was drinking and the fact that there was nothing else to watch on television for the next hour until Chris came home, my curiosity drove me to seek out the online application. The application was straightforward, simple questions about my background and a section to write why I would make a good business partner for Lord Sugar. In total I spent 15 minutes applying. Pressing submit, I did not think much about it again and got back to my glass of wine.

Fast-forward three months when I received a call from the executive producer of *The Apprentice*. Chris and I were just about to sit down to eat a bowl of warm soup for lunch when the call came. It was still blisteringly cold outside, the last part of a long winter that year. The producer slowly explained that they had chosen me as a candidate for season 14 of *The Apprentice*. On the call I was delighted, but after I hung up, I recall looking at Chris and immediately saying: 'I can't really do this, can I?'

After I had submitted my application, I had spent a couple of months going through the audition process so the acceptance call was not totally out of the blue. But I had not actually considered the possibility of going on the show and what that might mean. I had spent the past 15 years in London clawing my way to the top, building and then selling my business. People were finally taking me seriously. I had board positions and earned a significant sum for keynote speaking gigs all around the world. I had finally achieved a morsel of success and was riding that wave both financially and professionally. Was I really going to throw all that away for a chance to compete on a reality television show?

Unlike most candidates, it was the competition alone which compelled me to consider being a candidate. I did not desire to be on television, nor did I care about winning the £250,000 on offer (although I would never turn down free money). Competitive by nature, I relished the chance to put my skills to the test among peers. Running a business at an early age meant I had never competed against work colleagues for the chance of a promotion. Nor did I have to compete in the boardroom; clients took my advice because they paid for it. In the office, employees took my advice because I paid them to take it. It became a vicious cycle that meant I lived in a bubble where it seemed I could do no wrong professionally. And that drove me crazy. My competitive nature meant that the chance to compete on a level footing with business tasks I had no experience in was like Christmas.

Chris and I sat at our kitchen table as our soup grew cold writing down a list of pros and cons of joining the show. The pros included the chance to gain a new experience, something to do in my Year of Yes, and all the free press invites to glitzy events following the show being aired (which never actually materialized!). The con being that there was a possibility I would lose all the credibility I had built if my involvement went south during filming.

If it had just been up to me, I think I might have chickened out and called the producer back to turn down the offer. However, Chris made a very salient point at the end of our discussion (we had moved onto wine by then), promising me: 'If it all goes horribly wrong, we could move to India for a year until it blows over.' A particularly good point to make.

Being a reality television show aficionado, I remembered that these shows and the journeys of the people on them are incredibly short-lived. Those 15 minutes of fame are truly brief. Even if I was the worst candidate in the history of the show, everyone was sure to forget about it the following year.

It was Chris's statement that convinced me. We were certainly not ruling out the fact that I might look like a complete moron. In fact, we expected it. Although neither of us had any experience in television, we were acutely aware that editing would secure my fate. With a career history of being outspoken, it was unlikely I would go unnoticed.

And yet I chose to put everything I had worked for on the line. I was ready to put my business reputation at the mercy of television producers I had never met and have my personal life ripped apart by the British public.

So why did I do it? Especially at a time when I did not need the money and had booked a year off to travel the world. I never expected to win, therefore the potential loss of credibility and outright embarrassment seemed to far outweigh any potential gains I was hoping to make.

This is precisely the reason that you do not see many successful businesspeople on reality television. Truthfully, there is not much in it for them. But in addition to little upside, there is fear.

A fear of failure, because once success has been achieved, there is even greater pressure to achieve more.

The risk of success is that it often begets a façade of success. People stop questioning your judgement because you have been successful in the past. You stop growing and start believing your own hype. You begin to speak about success as though you can predict it because you once achieved it. However, as we have seen through the examples in this book, including BrewDog and Kylie Cosmetics, success is not necessarily attributed to previous actions or experience. Instead it is driven by our ability to be agile and find solutions to new problems. Inevitably thinking bigger than the problem itself.

But being agile is not something that comes naturally. More importantly, how can you think bigger than the problem itself if you cannot even identify the problem in the first place?

As we outlined in Chapter 1, humankind's survival is based on identifying patterns in nature and repeating those patterns successfully. Mimicry is a skill we are familiar with, a skill we are adept at. A skill that has been passed down from generation to generation and so it becomes something easily utilized in our day-to-day lives. Stepping into the unknown without understanding the consequences is not only frightening, it goes against our very nature.

The ability to forge our own path, without seeing the consequences of those new roads, is completely foreign. As we saw with psychologist Albert Bandura and social cognitive theory, we are hardwired to also elicit patterns of behaviour after we have seen others elicit them – not just after we have learned them ourselves through experience. Therefore, action without experience requires a significant leap of faith.

But as we have discovered with the many examples in this book, it is this leap of faith that is required for new leadership to break boundaries. And boundaries must be broken to begin playing by the new set of rules in the future of work. It is this leap of faith that others have taken in business which has previously identified them as rebels, punks, mavericks and outliers. Fortunately, it is something we can all replicate with a bit more effort and humility in the event of failure.

The desire to do something despite our fear of failure gives us the experience we may be lacking in viewing the behaviour elsewhere. By executing action based on your self-belief system alone you will begin to cultivate your own experiences, which will propel you forwards. Regularly putting yourself, and your self-worth, in harm's way is the antidote to remaining stagnant. The antidote to ignorance. In a world where information is at our fingertips, it has become a necessity to utilize, integrate and assimilate the right information in as timely a manner as possible in order to take decisive action.

After Chris and I finished our glasses of wine, rather than call the producer back, we poured ourselves another and toasted to joining *The Apprentice*. With trepidation I made the decision, figuring the worst that could happen would land me in India for a year, one of my favourite places to travel.

I made it to week 9 of *The Apprentice*, getting fired just two episodes before the final. During that time, I built a name for myself. I was often commentated on by both the public and television presenters. I started the season with presenter Rhod Gilbert creating a segment on his show *The Apprentice: You're Fired* naming me 'The Opinionator', highlighting the backlash I received from the British public for being 'too aggressive'. Fortunately, it was not all negative. I received some great praise from one of Lord Sugar's aides, Claude Littner, the British business executive famous on the show for his mercilessly tough interview style, who later called me 'brilliant'.

As I expected, being on the show did not advance my career and in many cases became more of a challenge. My speaking agent put it bluntly by telling me: 'We have been pitching and booking you as an *expert*. By going on a show called *The Apprentice*, we can't pitch you as one anymore.'

Unfortunately, she was right. Although I gained thousands of followers on social media, my paid speaking gigs dwindled. But in the grand scheme of it all, I did come out unscathed. We did not have to move to India and my life went back to normal almost immediately after the final episode aired in December 2018.

I thoroughly enjoyed my time in the process, but if you ask me what I learned from taking on the actual tasks, I would say it was minimal – aside from finding out that you really do have to wake up at 4 am and, much to my disappointment, they do not provide you with someone to do your hair and make-up. I did however walk away with a revolutionary new take on how television, specifically reality television, is made. I found it fascinating. Although this has not come in handy yet, I anticipate it will. Like Kylie Jenner who would not have guessed that perfecting her pout on Instagram would build her an empire, I see my time on the show as part of a larger puzzle of new skills and experiences that I need to acquire for the future. I would do it again in a heartbeat.

Looking back on that winter evening in November on my sofa, I could have just kept watching television. I could have just poured another glass of pinot noir. Most people would have. It is far easier and much less risky to not put yourself out there. To not risk the fear of utter failure and venture into the unknown. It is certainly much easier to launch new opportunities when there is nothing to lose. But when there is something to lose, the drive towards advancement through experience diminishes.

This is a problem because it does not support the necessary growth of new leadership skills within the future of work. In order to continue evolving and maintaining your edge, you must act rebelliously in the sense that you are willing to take that leap of faith into the unknown *in order* to learn new lessons and gain new skills. We need these skills to remain relevant and be valuable to those we work with because getting to the top is no longer as safeguarded as it once was. We must remain active in maintaining leadership. This is good for everyone but does put a lot more pressure on leadership learning. Complacency is no longer an option.

Another female leader who understands the concept of taking risks in the future of work is British technology entrepreneur Alex Depledge MBE. Venturing into the complete unknown, she left her stable job as a consultant at Accenture to co-found Hassle in 2012, a London-based online platform for domestic cleaners. After securing significant funding from the first backers of Facebook and Spotify, she sold the company just three years later for £27 million.[1] Her quick rise made her a star on Britain's start-up scene, a platform where she is known for telling it like it is and throwing out the rule book. In an article for *Management Today* she writes:

> Entrepreneurs have to be willing to take risks and embrace the unknown. They need to get things done without any structure and thrive in an environment where there are no rules. They need courage to innovate and the nerve to forge their own path – even armed with the knowledge there's a chance they might be pouring their and other people's money down the plughole.[2]

This stance can easily be taken by one who has found success early on, but Depledge proves she is not a hypocrite. Rather than ride the coat-tails from Hassle she took a second leap into the unknown to launch online architectural platform Resi just two years later. As Depledge puts it: 'We have to foster an attitude that anything is possible and that failure and cock-ups are all part of a learning curve.'[3]

Unfortunately, not everyone can be as brave as Depledge without help. But armed with some simple tricks to help you avoid the pitfalls of complacency you too can foster new habits to help you keep pushing boundaries. The trick is to keep going.

Now that we have built the foundations of passion and purpose learned from the previous chapters, we can utilize that drive to help us take the necessary leap into the unknown.

Using data to avoid sandbagging

Sandbagging is a strategy to 'lower down expectations of the company or strength of an individual to relatively produce greater results than actually projected'.[4] Put simply, it is the action to under-promise knowing that you will over-deliver. It allows everyone to pat themselves on the back. This concept is often utilized by salespeople to showcase a consistent sales effort throughout the year. When sales are going well, they push closing deals to the following quarter to help even out lack of confidence or dips in performance. This tactic can also be utilized by financial controllers to manage investor expectations, providing themselves a safe range to operate within. Sandbagging is common, extremely common. So common in fact that most people just assume that sandbagging is utilized within all companies and therefore the fields have been levelled regardless.

Unfortunately, the strategic drive to implement average so that it looks like success blocks both the company and the individual from maximizing their true potential. Furthermore, it has become so commonplace that many companies and individuals are doing it without even realizing it. The issue is that the consequences of sandbagging are significant.

Sandbagging has evolved into mainstream business because of the over-abundance of participation ribbons given out in school. When everyone gets a medal, an unconscious link between the act of sheer participation and happiness is formed. Later in life, achievement becomes a necessary adult replacement for school participation. Achievement based on constant reward is why sandbagging is so prevalent and is an accepted rule of good business practice. But as before, old rules need to be broken for us to achieve greater success as a leader in the future of work.

To understand how to avoid sandbagging in greater detail we look to sport.

THE NFL REGIONAL COMBINES KEEP US FRESH

In February each year at the Lucas Oil Stadium in Indianapolis over 335 college footballers participate in a week-long showcase of physical and mental standardized testing known as the NFL Regional Combines. These footballers are not just any footballers; they represent the All-American dream and have trained their whole lives to run drills including the 40-yard dash and pump out as many repetitions of the 225-pound bench press they can muster. It is competition at its peak, and it is brutal. The results of this evaluation process determine an athlete's future, or lack thereof, depending on how each measures up.

Despite criticism from sports writers and research analysts who question the validity of future player performance based on Combine performance, this 40-year-old programme gains more popularity each year. So much so that the Scouting Combine has extended not only to other regions in the United States, but also internationally. In one year, Combine evaluation will test up to one thousand of the world's top athletes.

Although one can align similarities between the short-termism of this one shot in a Combine to that of a job interview, what is more telling are the numbers behind the evaluation format. Considering that at any given point only 1,696 players are playing in the NFL each year there is a possibility to replace 20 per cent of current athletes with new athletes. The fear that a younger, more athletic, better version can come up the ranks swiftly through a Regional Combine ensures that professional players remain at the top of their game by indirectly reminding drafted players that they are disposable.

The fear of being replaced becomes a main driver towards consistently overperforming. The drive to put their bodies, their health and in many cases their minds on the line each Sunday is motivated by the all too real knowledge that every game might be their last. Sandbagging does not occur in a situation like this because performance is not managed as one would manage expectations in a job or within sales figures. One poor performance or even one average performance could mean the end of their career.

This exceptionally visible and present competition does not exist in the business world. While we might be aware of other people vying for our jobs within an organization, they are often few and far between. Outside of our work life, we engage in competition on minor scales such as where our children go to school or how much money we make compared to our friends. We never experience the fear of absolute crushing competition. And we have designed it that way. We avoid fear like the plague. We have become so sensitive to our fear of failure that we forget that failure can also provide an opportunity for us to learn.

This is why sandbagging is so prevalent. It is a coping mechanism to living life. However, the problem with sandbagging in the future of work is that it will never produce exceptional results because you will never overperform at anything if you are only constantly driving towards average.

Making it more problematic is that it is often hard to recognize when our actions are driven out of fear of failure. We have become so used to being driven to do a good job that we often take it for granted. Therefore, to avoid sandbagging, you must set goals that are beyond what you know you can easily achieve. By setting goals you will fail at, motivation drivers shift. As the NFL Regional Combine has proven, providing scarcity and competition is enough to ensure that each player is kept on their toes and performing to the best of their ability. Just like the quarterback of a team does not set a goal for each game on how many touchdowns he is going to complete, the same goes for your personal limits being confined to your annual salary or hours worked. Giving your best does not necessarily need to be measured, as long as you are able to continue the output each and every day of the week.

However, without competition to drive you forward this is an impossible task because most of us lack the motivation to work this hard all the time. So we need to rely on some tricks to assess our own capabilities in order to ensure we continue to drive towards the goals we have set.

This is where data comes in.

No matter if you are a doctor, a stay-at-home parent or a tech geek you will have aspirations that have yet to be realized. At the same time, you have likely clocked up achievements that you value. This is the start of your own data set. Begin by looking at where you have found success and analyse it. Was it based on what you thought you could achieve? If so, you need to assess whether you could have done better. And if you could have done better, what information would you have needed to do so? By analysing what you have done previously you can begin to assess how you might progress moving forward.

For example, a company I invested in and sit on the board of loves a good sandbag. In fact, they run their entire company in this way. They consistently present great figures showing how they achieve every financial goal. The board directors nod in agreement while I diplomatically try to explain the issues and my concern that we are not pushing fast enough. I outline that while hitting targets is fundamentally a good thing (I most certainly would be less impressed if they had not met their targets), their ability to hit every financial target each month means they are not doing much to push the boundaries beyond what they are capable of. I do not need to point this out. The data illustrates this. They are far from failures, but it is because they have not done anything in which they might fail. They consider themselves an ambitious company but have not set ambitious goals. When their goals and actions do not align, their expectations (and mine as a shareholder and board director) are unlikely to come to fruition. Their dream of being revolutionary is likely to be replaced by average at best because working in such a way drives underperformance.

This also causes issues for employees of leaders who sandbag. Not only does it create precedence for employees to actively sandbag their own goals and achievements, but it can be demotivating when the leader who is supposed to inspire you is settling for average. Regardless of whether sandbagging is discussed (or even known by the leader who is using it), it is something that can be felt across a company. Employees show up to work because it is their day job, not because they are inspired to do something great.

Ironically, the process of using sandbagging to gain recognition for achievement kills any chance of making real achievement or progress possible. A leader in the future of work cannot inspire a company by being average and therefore attracts employees who are happy to settle. But as we have outlined earlier in the book, the future generation is no longer interested in settling. They know what else is out there and they want more. It is up to a leader to ensure they can deliver, and sandbagging is not the answer.

Fortunately, this can be avoided by reviewing the data. Look at your company projections – are you meeting every target set? If so, you are likely sandbagging. On a personal level you also need to analyse the data in your life. Have you managed to attain everything relatively easily, but still feel unfulfilled? If so, you may be coasting. You need to instil a bit of fear and a little self-motivation to push beyond your boundaries. Not everyone has the fear of hundreds of ambitious Lycra-wearing men trying to take their job like the football players in the NFL do, but trust me, they are out there. Just because you cannot see them does not mean you should take your foot off the gas.

Futureproof your skills and adapt to permanent change

One way to ensure complacency does not set in is to constantly upskill. With unlimited access to information our ability to do this has never been easier. While this is a good thing, it also means that the usefulness of a skill learned has dramatically fallen through advancement in all areas of work. Today the half-life of a skill has fallen to just five years.[5] This means that a skill you learned for career progression will only be relevant to you during the time that it drives innovation, usually in the first few years of you learning it. Unfortunately, that skill quickly becomes irrelevant in just five years. In less than 10 years the skill you had hoped would carry you throughout your illustrious career will have absolutely no value at all, making it obsolete to your future.

If this thought alone is grim, it is made even more so by the fact that people are living longer. For the first time in history most people can expect to live well beyond their sixties. With over 125 million people currently aged 80 years or more, we are already living through and managing the effects of an ageing population. But take note: what we are seeing is nothing compared to what is to come. This ageing population has significant implications in the future of work. By 2050 'the world's population aged 60 years and older is expected to total 2 billion, up from 900 million in 2015'.[6] In the same year it is projected that 125 million people aged 80 years or older will be living in China alone, with 434 million people in this age group worldwide – four times greater than what we currently manage. It would be naive to expect all these people to remain on the golf course.

Therefore if the half-life of a skill has fallen to five years, compounded by the fact that we are extending our career timeline due to an ageing population, then we would have to re-train 12 times over the course of a 60-year career. This is radically different from what we have ever seen. In the past a skill was expected to carry you your entire career. If you were lucky, that career could be passed down for generations to follow.

Transportation is a great example of how innovations are exponentially shortening the half-life of being a driver. The first report of a horse-drawn carriage was in 1900 BC, which eventually was replaced by taxis in 1897. This means that the skill to driving a horse-drawn carriage lasted for 3,797 years. Long enough to last for generations, which is why this skill was passed down and often remained in the family. Unfortunately, taxis did not have as long a run and only utilized their skill for 120 years until they were competing with Uber. With an even shorter fate, Uber is projected to be out of business once the self-driving cars of the future become widely available effectively making the job of being a driver completely irrelevant in the future.[7]

But it is not just individuals who are feeling the squeeze of the shortening lifespan of skills. The same thing is happening with jobs and entire businesses. For example, social media managers were some of the most sought-after jobs when they first arrived in 2007 but have quickly been replaced by automation, allowing more people to manage their own social media accounts. You no longer need to hire a full-time social media expert to join your team; instead you can sign up to HubSpot.

Businesses are also feeling the pinch. A study produced by Credit Suisse in 2017 has shown that 'in the 1950s the average lifespan of a business was 60 years but, today, it is less than 20 years'.[8] This is all down to disruption at a speed we have never witnessed. At the current churn rate it is likely that half of S&P 500 companies will be replaced over the next 10 years.[9] These shrinking business lifespans are partly driven by technology shifts, but more often are due to companies missing opportunities to adapt and take advantage of changes through economic innovation. We have already seen this play out with L'Oréal and the beauty industry earlier in the book, but it is a trend that is impacting all sectors and acts as a barometer for the marketplace change we are currently experiencing. Stronger leadership with an understanding of staying ahead of the curve is necessary to ensure both jobs and businesses can evolve. It then becomes a leader's prerogative to learn as much as they can about specific threats and opportunities on a global scale. They must not only accept that a transformation is required, but also be ready to act on it.

Although upskilling to stay ahead as an inherent part of your lifestyle may seem daunting, unfortunately you do not have a choice.

As we have witnessed, the pace of change is not slowing and the quicker you can get on the bandwagon to integrate continuous learning into your daily life, the quicker you will be at keeping up and managing change effectively.

Fortunately there are tricks you can adopt to help prepare yourself for a lifetime of education, regardless of whether you are an employee, a student or a CEO.

1 **Start a blog.** Writing that is shared is not just a form of therapy, but a process of integrating new information and consolidating that information for others. Reading alone is not enough because most people are unable to integrate the learned principles into their actual work; however, when you pair reading with the act of sharing you are forcing yourself to learn what you read. This active form of learning happens because most people are too afraid to say the wrong thing in a public forum. By writing a blog that is available for everyone to access, you are instilling a level of responsibility for yourself and the information you are sharing. By taking a more considered approach you will enhance your ability to retain that information.

   You do not need huge set-up costs to do this. The point is to ensure your ideas are shared in a public forum. If that means you post your blog on a LinkedIn group or on your own website, the results are the same and will ensure you remain relevant.

2 **Learn a new skill.** You cannot predict the future, but you can arm yourself with new skills. Online education has evolved dramatically and there is now the opportunity to take part in coursework on demand from massive open online course providers. These virtual courses are short, broad-ranging and cheaper than traditional classroom education. With over 20

million new learners signing up for at least one online course each year, this is not a new trend.[10] From personal development to health sciences, there is an opportunity to upskill in almost any area of education – available in the comfort of your own home at a time that suits you best. I personally have enjoyed learning more about finance and investing in order to help supplement my knowledge of business in general.

But online learning is not the only way you can gain a new micro-credential. Many open universities such as General Assembly offer evening courses and programmes to fit your lifestyle for both companies and individuals. Just because you may be a postman by day does not mean you cannot learn to code by night.

It is also important to note that learning new skills should be approached not necessarily with the aim of achieving a higher pay-cheque in your current role, but that the skill learned is a stepping stone to increasing your ability to solve complex problems in the future. Gaining a micro-credential in coding will not be the gateway to a six-figure salary at Google; however, it may help you secure your next job which may lead to a future in technology.

Approach learning as part of life and make it a habit. Skills need to be gained for general advancement, not specific achievement.

3   **Take up any opportunity.** Upskilling and retraining do not need to be done with certification in mind but should be undertaken with the desire to access new opportunities and new people. Get out of your comfort zone and do something you have not done before. Whether that means swapping your annual all-inclusive trip basking in the Mexican sun for a week building houses in Guatemala or helping your friend launch a drinks product at a music festival for a free ticket, there is no shortage of things to do – and yet we regularly find ourselves doing the same thing year after year

In 2019 I met Dr Jane Galton who is a trustee of the Cheetah Conservation Fund UK, a charity that increases awareness and implements conservation programmes to protect cheetahs in the wild. With less than the time it took me to finish my cappuccino over our first meeting, I had signed up to volunteer at the Cheetah Safe House in Hargeisa, Somaliland, a few weeks later. I spent a week building shelters and feeding cheetahs. It was an incredible experience. Although I do not anticipate I will ever launch a business with big cats, what I learned about charities, business in Africa and wildlife conservation in that one week was invaluable.

By not exposing yourself to new experiences, you will find gaining new skills that much harder. Make change a regular part of your life and the learning will come much more naturally.

Goal setting in the context of evaluation

Many leadership books discuss goal setting, but very few discuss it in the context of implementation. Having a goal is great, but without a realistic execution plan they remain vision boards that fade like the poster of New Kids on the Block above my childhood bed.

Before we explore how to create effective goal pathways, it is important to first outline two ways to create goals in the first place: SMART goals and OKRs.

SMART goals

SMART goals are the most basic of the two. They provide a clear directive for setting goals and usually help people with big ideas but little clarity. Many people start off goal setting with lofty ideas such as 'I want to be a millionaire' or 'I want to run a tech company that rivals Google'. While these are certainly goals, they provide little substance to measure against. SMART provides the criteria to set goals with clear objectives so you know when they have been achieved.

To make your goal SMART, you need to ensure it meets the following criteria:

- **Specific:** Ensure your goal is well defined, clear and unambiguous.
- **Measurable:** Your goal must be quantifiable for you to track progress or success.
- **Attainable:** Is your goal realistic and do you have the tools and/or resources to attain it?
- **Relevant:** Does your goal align with your values and self-belief system?
- **Timely:** There must be a deadline to achieve your goal.

From the example above, you could turn a lofty objective into a SMART goal in the following ways: 'I will become a millionaire by the time I am 30 years old by setting up my own profitable business this year in the cat food industry.' By all standards this qualifies as a SMART goal:

- **Specific:** I want to become a millionaire.
- **Measurable:** Setting up a profitable business.
- **Achievable:** Technically anyone can set up a business.
- **Relevant:** Passion for cat food.
- **Timely:** By the time I am 30.

The issue with SMART goals is that even though the goal is defined, it is still not clear enough to help link a lofty ambition to the day-to-day execution of achieving that ambition.

OKRs go a bit further.

OKRs

OKRs is the acronym for Objectives and Key Results. It is a framework extensively used in Silicon Valley start-up culture as it was central to Google's management methodology, but it originated at Intel in the 1970s. Although it is predominantly used by corporates (LinkedIn, Twitter, Uber, Zynga, Motorola, Netflix, Code for America to name a few) it can also be used for personal development and by individuals looking to get things done in organizations where senior leadership does not use any goal setting.

What makes OKRs go further is the fact that they are iterative and collaborative. Rather than set out one goal, it becomes a framework for tracking progress, creating alignment and encouraging engagement. The value of this framework is that goals are *shared*. This enables straightforward navigation along the inevitably bumpy road that lies ahead. Having a north star is crucial for any leader, but having that north star shine a light on the path to get there is what will make or break your success.

Fortunately, OKRs are quite simple. They comprise an objective which is the clearly defined goal, along with one or more key results specified over a defined period, alongside measures used to track the achievement of that goal. While setting the right objective is important, key results are what make OKRs work. These are numerically based progress success points that drive you closer to achieving the objective. In a way they are the mini objectives that allow you to achieve the larger objective. They begin to outline the execution pathway and allow you to analyse the data objectively.

For example, your objective could be: grow the global business. To align that lofty objective with measurable action points your key results could include:

- hit company annual global sales target of $100 million;
- achieve 100 per cent year-on-year sales growth in EMEA;
- increase company deal size by 30 per cent before the end of the year;
- hire one new sales director in Asia.

If the key results are achieved easily then the numerical goal attached to it was not aggressive enough, as we saw earlier with sandbagging. Alternatively, if you are unable to achieve any of your key results then you need to revise expectations and discuss capabilities. At Google, teams that use OKRs strive to achieve a 0.6–0.7 score against stated objectives.[11] This means that they aim to achieve only 60–70 per cent of their key results. It is an indicator for how hard they are pushing.

As Larry Page, co-founder of Google, puts it: 'OKRs have helped lead us to 10x growth, many times over. They have helped make our crazily bold mission of "organizing the world's information" perhaps even achievable. They've kept me and the rest of the company on time and on track when it mattered the most.'[12]

If it is good enough for Larry, it is good enough for me.

Developing the implementation pathway

While OKRs set key results you can measure yourself against frequently, you still need to think of the plan you will set out to reach those key results. Everyone has different skill sets, different networks and different opportunities – as they say, there is more than one way to skin a cat. You need to develop the path that works best for you.

With thousands of blogs outlining tips and tricks, these should not be implemented verbatim. What works for one person does not necessarily work for the next. Your execution strategy should be specific to your skill set, your interests, and aligned to your personal ambition. Having a goal is just one part of the equation. Without the right execution it just remains an ambition. While many people have goals and ambitions, far fewer achieve them due to inaction and poorly structured planning. The tools are not only at your fingertips, the tools are at everyone's fingertips, which makes the process of developing your own path both liberating and terrifying.

Once you have decided on an execution strategy to reach your goals, you must implement it and learn from it. You will never get it right the first time. The trick is learning how to bounce back quickly from setbacks and learn from all-out failure. By viewing the process of building your pathway as an iteration rather than the 400m sprint, you will cultivate each step with purpose and analytical consideration. The world is changing too fast to clearly see the best next steps to take, so being open to iteration is essential.

This chapter has reinforced the things we need to do now. We have discovered that leadership no longer means delegating from an isolated ivory tower. We ourselves must act. In a world where information is everywhere, competition is fiercer than ever. But by utilizing action as a form of learning you can keep complacency at bay and continue to remain invaluable, both now and in the future.

Having laid a strong foundation to unleash the rebel within to think beyond rules governed by the status quo, we are now ready to look towards the future.

What does the future of work look like and how can we be an active part in its evolution, rather than constantly feeling the fear of catching up? To answer that question, we look to hip-hop.

PART THREE

The future

CHAPTER SEVEN

The future is collaborative

Defying all odds

To make Apple history is no mean feat, but to find it was done by the most unlikely of pairs is what makes this story fascinating.

At just 5 ft 5 in Jimmy Iovine is diminutive. But do not let his size fool you. What Iovine may lack in stature he more than makes up for in charisma and enthusiasm. Climbing the music industry corporate ladder to become the chairman of Interscope, the US umbrella label owned by Universal Music Group, he started his career mopping floors in a recording studio. A testament to his talent and ambition. Following an illustrious career and entertaining personal life which included dating Stevie Nicks of Fleetwood Mac fame, he is known throughout the music industry as one of the most dynamic men in the business.

A dramatic contrast, Andre Romelle Young, known as Dr Dre, towers above most at 6 ft 1 in. Unlike Iovine, who spent his childhood around Italian dinners in Brooklyn, Dr Dre was raised in a housing project in Compton, California, by his grandmother. Finding fame with the influential gangster rap group N.W.A, which popularized explicit lyrics in rap to detail the violence of street life, he is soft spoken and known for being a perfectionist.

In the lead-up to the pair's first meeting, Dr Dre was already a legend – known for being one of the driving forces in hip-hop. Having famously left N.W.A after a financial dispute, he managed to get out of his contract early to set up Death Row Records, which subsequently discovered Tupac Shakur. But it was *The Chronic* album that set him on the path to what inevitably became his legacy and the reason Dr Dre found himself in front of Iovine in 1992.

Although Death Row Records produced his first solo album, *The Chronic*, Dr Dre needed a distributor. With several lawsuits following him around, the main distributors who would have normally released his record would not touch it. It was far too complicated; the financial risks were too high. Having run out of viable options, Dr Dre found himself at Interscope, a record label known for producing rock music. Unsurprisingly, Iovine had never even heard of Dr Dre before he stepped into his office.

What caught Iovine's attention was the music. As Iovine puts it: 'Dre's sonics were far superior to any rock record being made, or any hip-hop. It just sounded better than anything else on my speaker.'[1] The unique sound was something Iovine noticed immediately, an ability to spot talent so remarkable that *Rolling Stone* magazine credits him as 'the man with the magic ears'.[2] But it wasn't just the sound that caught Iovine's attention. The fact that *The Chronic* was produced by sneaking into studios for fear of lawsuits catching up to Dr Dre prompted Iovine to dream big. He recalls thinking: 'Wow. If you can do it under those circumstances, let's go.'[3] It became a defining moment for Interscope and his career to jump when no one else would.

The Chronic became a pivotal partnership and set in motion a wave of successful music career launches to follow, including Snoop Dogg, Eminem, 50 Cent and Busta Rhymes. Over time, their reign in hip-hop founded an incredibly tight friendship between the two, which Iovine credits as key to their successes. In a *GQ* interview in 2014, Iovine says:

> That's really a special thing. We trust each other implicitly. It's the closest to a band as I was ever in. We know what each other does, and we trust each other's instincts so much, that when he's moving somewhere and I go, 'No', he goes, 'OK, let's not do that.'[4]

In a dog-eat-dog industry where the top dog rules, this is refreshingly honest.

Even the award-winning documentary *The Defiant Ones*, which profiles their friendship and culminates with the sale of their Beats headphones company, was originally supposed to be a solo film on Dr Dre's life.[5] However, Dr Dre's friendship with Iovine was such an obvious foundation for his life's work that HBO was compelled to weave Interscope into its storytelling. The film documents how they serendipitously launched Beats by Dre – headphones with a difference. The idea originated from an initial endorsement for sneakers. Iovine thought bigger and prompted the rapper to switch into a product that was more in line with his interests – sound. Specifically, headphones. But unlike the thousands of endorsement deals that had come before, Iovine convinced the rapper to combine their expertise and love of sound to make headphones together, under a new business they would run together. It sounded simple. It *was* simple. But it is worth recognizing that although both had illustrious careers in the music industry and produced many world-charting albums from scratch, neither had ever owned, created or launched a consumer product before. This was uncharted territory and is a great example of how they pushed themselves beyond their comfort zones – a fundamental new rule in the future of work which we explored in the last chapter.

To bring on the hardware expertise required, 'Beats by Dre' headphones were launched in partnership with boutique audio manufacturing company Monster Cable Products. The product hit the shelves in 2008. Characterized with more bass than their competitors, the headphones were optimized for hip-hop and pop music with an aim to influence culture.

The company continued using collaboration as a business strategy. Most apparent was its infiltration into their marketing which relied on both of their high-profile networks. Beats by Dre headphones were endorsed by the top pop and hip-hop musicians at the time and regularly seen in music videos.

After years of substantial growth, the company launched Beats Music in January 2014. This subscription-based online music streaming service utilized algorithm-based personalization, allowing users to listen to the right music at the right time. Shortly after the launch of Beats Music, Apple announced their purchase of the entire organization, including the streaming service and Beats Electronics which manufactures the headphones, for $3 billion – a deal that consisted of $2.6 billion in cash, the rest in Apple stock. The largest purchase in Apple's history.

There are a lot of lessons to learn from this, all which reinforce that old rules need to be broken in the future of work. At its foundation, Dr Dre and Iovine built a business that was aligned to their individual passion – sound. With absolutely no experience in product development, they brought in partners to fill in the skills gap and support promotion. Their network then amplified the message of providing a superior end-to-end music experience. Core to this amplification was its simplicity. Much like Greta Thunberg with her cardboard sign, it was its simplicity which started a movement by allowing others to easily connect to their common goal. Apple did not just buy a pair of headphones; they purchased a bit of culture.

The fact that they achieved something together that neither could have achieved alone is critical. This is not an outlier case.

It is a defining business case in the future of work. Fundamentally driven by an effective partnership that tapped into the strengths of both individuals, fuelled further by networks of influence.

Do not confuse this with influencer marketing. What we are unveiling goes well beyond that. The new rules of business that can easily be navigated by future rebellious leaders speak directly to the foundations of how business structures should be built by stressing the invaluable importance of others. The ability to tap into partnerships is no longer a cost-saving decision; it is a decision based on how much further a brand or an individual can go. No one is good at all things. By using a partner, whether that involves two individuals in the case of Beats by Dre or an organization like Seed Cosmetics and Kylie Jenner, you can achieve more together. This is no longer just a fact, but a fundamental shift defining the way of the future. You need to get on board (with others) or risk falling behind.

It may seem like these successful partnerships are few and far between, but in truth they are quickly becoming the norm. Unsurprisingly, Alex Depledge launched Hassle with a partner in crime whom she later joined up with when they launched Resi. These partnerships underpin success.

Although we have discussed them in the context of start-ups, the ability to create successful partnerships exists in traditional businesses as well. It is important to remember that what makes collaboration so successful is not the act of collaborating itself, but the action of co-creation – having multiple parties actively involved in the creation of a project or concept. Within an organization, this can be done with internal teams, by seeking out collaboration opportunities with different departments, or even by launching new projects with other companies.

Throughout this book we have discovered the value of partnerships, but we need to view them as a necessity rather than a 'nice to have'. The fast pace of change combined with the need to stay ahead of the curve requires help. We must utilize others.

Collaboration in this context is the act of working with other people and should not be confused with taking advice from other people, which we outlined earlier in the book as a rule to be broken. Where advice and being told what to do are passive, collaboration is active. It enables workflow to become integrated with other people's actions, thoughts and ideas. It is the key to unlocking the future of work as we now know it.

Partnerships required to change the world

I recall first hearing about the coronavirus on my way out the door in December 2019. As I fumbled by the coat rack putting on the many layers of scarves and sweaters that would protect me from the chill, my husband Chris casually mentioned something about a pandemic in China. As I was running late, I did not pay too much attention, instead making a joke about the stock value of Corona beer as I rushed out. It was not until a couple of months later that things really hit home. Shortly after it became a regular news feature, I found myself donning a medical mask and rubber gloves in Heathrow airport awaiting one of the last flights back to Vancouver, Canada. We had spent the last 48 hours frantically packing up our home in fear that they would shut all borders for the foreseeable future. Even if borders were not shut there seemed a very real possibility that airlines would grind to a halt or go bankrupt.

Perhaps the rash decision to leave would not have been made if we were on our own, but our circumstance of being eight months pregnant meant we wanted to ensure we had the support of our families back in Canada when the baby arrived. We could not take the chance of being stuck.

On a micro level Covid-19 changed our plans drastically, but on a macro level it has affected the world as we now know it. The world will never go back to what we knew as normal. While the origins of the virus remain unclear, it is believed that in late

2019 someone was infected with the virus by an animal at a wet market in Wuhan. By April 2020 it had spread to nearly every country in the world. Compared with death tolls of other global epidemics, Covid-19, which by December 2020 had killed over 1.47 million people, is worse than Swine Flu (H1N1) which killed 575,400 people, but significantly less devastating than HIV/AIDS (43.8 million dead) or the Spanish Flu (50 million dead).[6]

Many countries were in lockdown with populations self-isolating in their homes. Schools shut, businesses closed, parks were inaccessible; life as we knew it felt over. The restlessness was palpable and despite solace in the form of an Oklahoma man with a meth addiction and 180 pet tigers documented on Netflix, people demanded a timeline for when sheltering at home would be over. But the only timeline that governments gave was that a vaccine would likely be available by the summer of 2021. And even that did not sound convincing.

After months of extraordinarily little information provided by governments about the virus, the vaccine or the projected length of self-isolation everyone must endure, big business finally took matters into its own hands. On 10 April 2020 two of the world's largest companies, Apple and Google, joined forces in an unprecedented collaboration to create a decentralized contact tracing tool to stop the spread of the coronavirus. Announced with a mission to 'harness the power of technology to help countries around the world slow the spread of Covid-19 and accelerate the return of everyday life', this further illustrates that isolated achievements are no longer enough.[7] The world's problems are too big for a single entity to solve alone. We must work together.

While we instinctively understand the effectiveness of working with partners we like, what the Google and Apple partnership proves is that achievement can also be driven through identifying a shared goal with those that we view as competitors or rivals. There is benefit beyond the personal enjoyment found working with a friend or colleague. There are significant opportunities for advancement to be realised by combining forces and skill sets. The joint effort of two of the biggest mobile operating systems, Android and iOS, is unmatched and their alliance will enable a reach of an estimated 3 billion people. It is a partnership difficult to replicate in scale with any other government or business. Competition aside, this very visible partnership will impact almost half of the entire world's population in an incredibly positive way. This is a real-world example of how the future of partnerships can fill the gap for the greater good when misplaced politics are side-lined.

Our desire to create positive impacts and change the world through our actions – which we discovered in Chapter 3 is fundamental to our desired state – is dissolving historical boundaries and breaking old rules. There is no longer a clear divide in business or in life. No longer layered secrets surrounded in isolation only uncovered on a need-to-know basis. Instead we have evolved into a state of shared learning. Of utilizing networks to work more effectively and efficiently. Collaborating to achieve a single goal, regardless of whether that partner competes for market share. We have proven we have progressed beyond the 'greed is good' mantra of the 1980s to the new rule book of the future where real change is finally happening. No longer branded disruptive, this is the new norm.

Ripping up the rule book in Old Hollywood

This new norm of wide-scale collaboration is not only seen in the technology sector (where you would expect it), but in traditional sectors with more entrenched reticence towards partnerships. One such sector not known for profit sharing is Hollywood, but mobile-only short-form streaming service Quibi managed to prove that creating new rules in Old Hollywood can be achieved.

Despite its momentous start, Quibi sadly was one of many start-ups to fall victim to Covid-19. Led by veteran executives Jeffrey Katzenberg and Meg Whitman, Quibi made headlines for raising nearly $1.8 billion for a concept many outlined as 'experimental' at best.[8] The service combined the high production quality of full-length feature films and television shows broken down into quick bites (qui-bi) – short chapters running 10 minutes or less. The idea was that this short-form content, much like YouTube videos, would be watched on the go. Although media companies had tried (and also failed) to launch something similar in the past, nothing had ever been done on the scale of Quibi. It was a gamble. And at a time when businesses were struggling with the pandemic, a gamble that did not pay off.

Just six months after its launch, Quibi was forced to shut down, reportedly returning $350 million of the money raised.[9] 'I attribute everything that has gone wrong to coronavirus,' Katzenberg told The New York Times. 'Everything. But we own it.'[10]

Although timing was not on their side, what makes this a topical and relevant business case is the structure of investors and the process of content creation. Both of which illustrate the future of partnerships. Surprisingly, both radical ideas were not to blame for the failure of the business. In fact, despite everything, the partnership structure was what ultimately drove this questionable business concept as far as it did.

Of the many investors that contributed a combined $1.8 billion, you would be surprised to discover almost all of them were direct competitors. Backers included the full suite of leading Hollywood studios including Disney, 21st Century Fox, NBCUniversal, Sony Pictures Entertainment, Viacom, AT&T's WarnerMedia (formerly Time Warner Inc), Lionsgate, MGM, ITV and Entertainment One – all corporations typically more comfortable fighting each other for talent and original storytelling than putting cheques into the same pot.[11] In the history of Hollywood there had never been another business in which all leading studios had invested together.

And it was not just cold hard cash they were committing; they were also partnering on content. Every studio that had invested into Quibi had also agreed to create new short-form content. Studios acted as both investors and suppliers in this complex collaboration with the common goal of bringing beautifully crafted storytelling to the device people use the most: the smartphone. This was the first subscription service without an archived library of content made possible through strategic collaboration. They understood that they could not achieve scale alone; they needed to rethink and reframe what they viewed as their network.

Reframing our view of the world as a network is critical in the future of work. The ability to see partnerships rather than competition is a decisive mindset and illustrates a clear strategic decision towards the future structure of businesses. The interesting thing about your competitors, whether in life or in business, is that they all share the same goal as you. Their direction, not necessarily their path, is more similar to yours than you might think. And as we identified in Chapter 4, shared objectives lay the foundation for collaborative-style leadership. Quibi proved this leadership concept works by partnering with some of the oldest businesses around. It seems old dogs can learn new tricks after all.

But partnership and collaboration in Quibi did not just end with big studios ensuring they remained relevant. In addition, Quibi created a new model of content ownership which forced shared profits with the content creators themselves, a radical departure from the past. Historically, studios owned the talent through long-term contracts. This monopolization left minimal shared upside for the actual creators – the directors, writers, actors and producers. Quibi forced the entire industry into a new conversation by utilizing a vastly different revenue model. Instead of Quibi owning the content in perpetuity like media studios of the past, they took the rebellious stance to *borrow* content.[12] Despite paying for production at a cost of $100,000/ minute – which far eclipses typical production costs on YouTube and other social media platforms – the company exclusively licensed its original series and movies for a limited time. The shows eventually reverted to their creators, who were then able to resell and repurpose the content back to Netflix or anyone else.

The structure of Quibi and its network of partners clearly demonstrates we are now ready to throw out the old rule book and replace it with collaborative leadership. Even traditional businesses are ready to start thinking differently about partnerships. Despite the fact that Quibi ended up being a blip in the streaming world, their revolutionary collaborative model will influence much of how content in the entertainment industry will be created in the future.

The partnerships we have outlined in this book offer just a glimpse into how the world is changing. Collaboration is not just beneficial; it is now fundamental as a solution to keep up with our radically shifting environment. To keep up with the pace of change, maintain our skills to drive innovation, and to harness the opportunities that now exist everywhere, we must work strategically with others. One person is not enough. The world is far too large to consume and navigate independently.

Choose partners wisely

If new rules dictate that we must harness the power of a network and collaborate with others, the next challenge is: how to do it sensibly. With the access and tools to partner with anyone, anywhere in the world, the opportunities are endless. However, it is not the simple act of working within a network or pulling pieces of the puzzle together that is the sole predictor of success. It is the ability to strategically align your goals with partners who often have quite different capabilities from your own. Again, this is easier said than done.

Despite director Woody Allen making a career storyboarding the theory that opposites attract, the truth is we are most attracted to people who are similar to ourselves. This extends beyond the simple laws of attraction and is often detrimentally played out in hiring scenarios. A recent study by Kellogg School of Management professor Lauren Rivera discovered that hiring is not just a process for skills sorting; it is also a process of cultural matching.[13] In the study, employers sought candidates who were perceived as culturally similar to themselves in terms of leisure pursuits, experiences and self-presentation styles. What becomes more telling is that any concern about shared culture often outweighed concerns about productivity or skill set. In effect, beyond age and gender, you are most likely to hire someone who shares your tastes, experiences and leisure pursuits. Hiring then becomes a process of matching people to pursue goals alongside someone identical to yourself.

While this may make work trips more bearable, it goes against the value collaboration can provide. The process of collaboration is to help expand critical thinking by considering new ideas. Therefore, people with different experiences and abilities will generate a much broader range of possibilities. Collaborators should broaden your discussions, not be the seal of approval for ideas you have already discovered.

Having a cheerleader is not only ineffective, it can be incredibly dangerous from an achievement perspective, making you susceptible to tunnel vision. We reviewed this when we examined complacency earlier in the book. Too often our desire to partner with someone likeminded leads us to partner with someone who has the same skill set and does not create diversity of thought, which is partly why between 40 and 70 per cent of joint ventures fail.[14]

To outline the dangers of collaboration and the common traps we often fall into when looking to create a partnership, we look to another riveting documentary in music.

Playing with Fyre

As we saw earlier with Robin Dunbar's research into network capacity, our ability to create real, meaningful connections is being challenged by our ever-increasing investment in online followers – resulting in feelings of loneliness on a global scale. To combat this, we desperately seek out physical bonding experiences that allow us to connect. As the world becomes more digital, this desire to bond grows proportionately.

And nothing is more bonding than music. Although it has always had the power to define culture by transcending boundaries, it is now being used to shape our identities. This need is driving the significant increase in festival attendance globally. In 2019 over 32 million people attended at least one music festival, half of the attendees being the most digitally native group of Millennials.[15] Music festivals are now a component of our lives, a new rite of passage.

Beyond the bonding experience itself, most music festivals are also fuelled by the need to create content for our social media feeds. Specifically, content that enables you to showcase a lifestyle of excess and luxury. Although social media posts of fringed vests and headdresses backstage are relatively new, the concept of music festivals to showcase elitism dates back hundreds of years. In the 19th century, festivals of classical music enabled the privileged to take pleasure in the finer things in life.[16] These classical music festivals have been captured in some of the world's most beautiful oil paintings such as *Orchestra Musicians* by Edgar Degas, one of the founders of Impressionism, as a way to boast. So, although boasting about affluence is not new, the frequency with which it now appears in culture via social media is.

Let us look at one of the more popular music festivals, the Coachella Valley Music and Arts Festival. Held annually in California in the Colorado Desert against a backdrop of sunshine and palm trees, Coachella makes an ideal location for those looking to fill their social media feeds. And festival-goers agree. In 2020 there were over 5 million posts tagged #Coachella on Instagram pre-coronavirus lockdown. While this is telling, it becomes more relevant when you compare the previous years. Just two years earlier in 2018 there were 2 million posts.[17] This increase over the last couple of years is noteworthy. With only 125,000 in attendance each year, the increase in posting behaviour per festival-goer has risen by 400 per cent in two years alone. Compare this to traditional media where a music festival would average a 10 per cent increase in marketing spend year-on-year. Its pervasive rise is shifting culture.

This trend amplifies short-termism at the expense of long-term security, especially for younger generations who are disillusioned with investing in material goods. Gone are the days when putting money aside to save up for a mortgage was the holy grail of adulting. As we have outlined earlier, future leaders have endured the financial crash. They now know there is no security in becoming a company man. They see life as fleeting. In this come-what-may type of lifestyle, short-term gains are personally more gratifying than holding out for long-term benefits that may never materialize. A recent Eventbrite study looked at the experience economy and discovered this viewpoint is held by the majority, with over 78 per cent of Millennials choosing to enrich their lives through experience and access over ownership.[18] Millennials want to live in the here and now.

Predictably this cultural drive paired with the advancement of technology and rise of the influencer has driven exponential commercial growth in the music festival industry. Capitalizing on culture, brands have driven the growth of these mass market events to significant profits, with over $1.34 billion spent annually by North American-based companies on sponsorship alone. Even festival organizers now have the capability to make an annual profit upwards of $100 million for each event.[19] As a result, everyone wants a piece of the pie.

As someone who has served up this music festival 'pie' for over two decades with a long-running career directing brands and festival organizers to the latest trends, Rebecca Jolly has had a front row seat to the evolution of the industry. Having worked across every type of music festival in practically every country in the world, including the life-impacting Tomorrowland which boasts over 14.7 million Facebook followers (by comparison Coachella has just 2.7 million), Jolly has seen the business shift from one of culture to one of profits and bank accounts. She does not like what she sees.

Driven by the rise of influencers and the instantaneousness of social media, music festivals have begun to shift from defining and creating culture to damaging culture. Jolly told me:

> People are mistakenly thinking that they can pay for culture without investing into it and developing it organically. They do not know the history, the blood, sweat and tears that went into years of building these festivals up to what they are now. People think they can just tap into the zeitgeist and shape it to fit their own objectives, but it just does not work like that. Culture needs to be carefully crafted, it is an art form, not a business plan.[20]

What Jolly alludes to is the fact that often the perception of quick fame and success through music festival acquisition is not the reality. By approaching it as such, organizers lose sight of the festival's *raison d'etre* – lacking purpose, it quickly loses what enticed fans in the first place.

Coachella is an excellent case in point. The mainstream popularity of Coachella gives the perception that this is a relatively new festival, one that is at the cutting edge. A trendsetter by any other means in the industry. But what many people do not know is that it has been going for over 20 years. Launched with just 37,000 people in October 1999 it was billed as 'the anti-Woodstock' by booking acts based on artistry rather than radio popularity.[21] With headline acts now including the likes of Beyoncé, it has clearly strayed far from its origins.

Jolly adds that the uncompromising focus on influence and influencers completely 'disregards the core purpose of music festivals in the first place', with brand sponsors aggressively infiltrating the stage line-up based on who has more online followers. Instead, they aim to exploit an opportunity to drive influence over cultural trends. With short-term thinking, their aim is to strike while the iron is hot and then move onto the next. And while brands can do this, and arguably should do this, what remains of the attendees and the organizers? If music festivals are core to our culture and the development of self-identity, what does this say about our future? Are we harming ourselves?

YOU NEED MORE THAN A SIZZLE REEL

Music festivals have laid the stage for identification, becoming big business in the process, but it is not just brands getting in on the action. Collaborators also want in. None so badly as young entrepreneur Billy McFarland and rapper Ja Rule.

In late 2016 McFarland and Ja Rule co-founded the now infamous Fyre Festival. Billed as a luxury music festival taking place on a private island in the Bahamas in April and May of 2017, it was launched as the hottest festival ticket one could get. Day tickets sold for up to $1,500 each and VIP packages that included airfare and luxury tent accommodation cost $12,000. By comparison, that year, a weekend pass to Coachella was only $429.

Heavily promoted on Instagram by bikini-clad influencers including Kendall Jenner, Bella Hadid, Hailey Baldwin and Emily Ratajkowski, the posts showcased private jets, blue waters, and 'the best in food, art, music and adventure'. It promised a transformative experience and tapped into the cultural hype of music festivals and social media influence at the time. These glitzy images did not just dupe the millions of viewers who saw the video pop up on their social media feed and the thousands who paid for tickets, but the hype also drove an offline following of over 100 investors to part with more than $26 million.[22] It became a movement. And with mere months between the launch announcement and the disaster that ensued on the 'greatest party that never was', there was little time to discover otherwise.

When the 5,000 ticket holders, a far cry from the 40,000 tickets projected in the business plan, arrived via school bus they were met with emergency tents for accommodation and wet cheese sandwiches. Quite contrary to the 'best in food, art, music and adventure' promised. But sadly this became the least of their problems when it was discovered upon arrival that nothing was set up. None of the stages had been built, no infrastructure was in place. In fact, nothing at all was built. Having paid upwards of $12,000, ticket holders were stuck on the island without food, water or shelter. A transformative experience it certainly was. As day rolled into evening, panic set in. Thousands took to mass hoarding of toilet paper and wet mattresses, captured in video snippets uploaded onto the social media networks they trusted to purchase tickets from just a couple of months prior. Not even the headline act turned up.

When questioned what her peers thought of the Fyre Festival fiasco, Jolly recounts that the entire music industry was sceptical from the first announcement. As she puts it: 'They might have had the sizzle with a well-produced promotional video and scantily clad models prancing around, but where exactly was the sausage?'

Where was the sausage is right. While we could review the fraudulent claims made by the duo, and much has been done since its disastrous conclusion culminating in a $100 million class action lawsuit and McFarland in jail for a six-year prison sentence in October 2018, what is most telling is how sour the partnership went – and how quickly. If collaboration is the future and finding the right partner is the pathway to success, how can you do so while avoiding the fate of Fyre Festival?

To understand this, we need to review many of the themes we have discussed in this book and utilize the learnings to reach a conclusion.

BREAK THE RULE OF COMPLACENCY

McFarland and Ja Rule met two years prior to launching Fyre Festival when McFarland was looking to book talent for his previous venture, card-based membership club Magnises (also discredited later as a scam). McFarland's first choice of artist to play at the event was Ja Rule, as he was a huge fan and said he had loved him since he was a kid. After an ordeal trying to book him (McFarland first approached Ja Rule through his Instagram account which unsurprisingly led him on a wild goose chase), he ended up having to fly Ja Rule out in a helicopter to play his gig.

Predictably the two grew close. McFarland seemed to have endless cash to spend on booking talent and Ja Rule, keen to perform gigs and fly in helicopters, was all too willing to be booked. Their bond, strengthened by the fact that they both dreamed of bigger pay-cheques, was fuelled by their quick-win attitudes towards success. Music festivals, with their A-list celebrity appeal and matching million-dollar profits, drew them like moths to a flame.

Little is known about whether there was any actual planning for the festival apart from a notebook found discarded onsite outlining orders needed for 6,000 packets of Skittles and 9,000 glow-lollipops.[23] In terms of experience, Ja Rule contends his trust in McFarland was built on other people's accounts of the entrepreneur, many describing McFarland as a 'child prodigy'.[24] Although 'child prodigy' would pique anyone's interest, it certainly is not a trait shared by festival organizers, more often found in the thick of details filling out planning permits than seen parading backstage popping bottles of champagne. Conversely McFarland seemed to think Ja Rule's celebrity appeal would be the only thing needed to add credibility to their bikini-clad showreel.

Apart from a handful of small gigs they had collaborated on, the two had extraordinarily little experience working together before announcing their lofty plans for Fyre Festival. There was no strategy for how their combined skill sets could be utilized for success.

Another red flag on their collaboration was the fact that McFarland and Ja Rule had zero experience in the product they were creating. And while new rules encourage us to get out of our comfort zone, collaboration teaches us to work with others who can help fill the gaps.

When Dr Dre and Iovine collaborated on Beats by Dre headphones, they did not set up their own manufacturing shop. Instead they initially collaborated with an audio and visual component manufacturer, Monster Cable, using their experience to collaborate with those who had the skills to create the product. By contrast, neither Ja Rule nor McFarland had organized a mass event and rather than hiring an expert team, focussed instead on promotion, spending millions of dollars. Understandably they focussed on the areas they had the most experience in, but as marketing and promotion is usually the last phase in creating a music festival, it became very clear they were in over their heads. The organizers had two months to set up what most small music festivals would take 18 months to plan. Their execution failed miserably because they were both ill-equipped to bring something like this together.

Although it was a disaster, it snowballed quickly into a catastrophe because of the cheerleading effect they had on each other. Where Ja Rule saw McFarland as an entrepreneurial genius despite all evidence to the contrary, McFarland did not want to let his idol down. Perhaps more astonishing is their continued confusion on where it all went wrong. Speaking at a marketing convention in November 2019 Ja Rule defended his vision by saying: 'If the festival would have been a success, they'd probably be teaching this marketing at colleges.'[25] Both Ja Rule and McFarland's desire to build a legacy greatly overcame common sense. The pair are a great example of how wrong haphazard partnerships can go.

Collaborate for good

Rebellious leadership is not simply the act of defying the status quo for the hell of it. Rebellious leadership means independently thinking and applying real-world experiences to your future endeavours. Utilizing your unique skill set and partnering with others who bring out the best in you to achieve more than you could alone. It is pushing the boundaries with the support of others. It is achieving more together.

But these are just words on a page. They are relatively useless without the blueprint for enabling successful collaboration to happen. We need to look at the steps to launch a collaboration and the keys to partnering with the right party to unlock potential.

We reviewed a framework and the importance of developing your passion in Chapter 5. As a reminder, leadership is no longer handed down from a generation or a corner office. It is now earned – driven independently by individuals anywhere in the world, even while sitting on pavement steps in Sweden. Passion is the fundamental step for any action taken in the future of work. It is your passion, communicated to the world, that becomes the spark that sets everything alight. It defines your purpose. Without it you will be unable to collaborate effectively because others will be unable to understand how they fit in.

Assuming we have done the work to define our passion and we have set the pace for our goals, it then becomes important to look to our networks. Collaborators and partners can be discovered everywhere. They can be life-long friends like Iovine and Dr Dre or they can be family members like M.92. They can also be strategic business partners like Seed Cosmetics and Kylie Jenner. The main point is that these collaborations are long-term relationships. This is not a quick fix to make more money. This is not a framework for an influencer #ad campaign. This is a framework for building a legacy.

Long-term collaboration is a solution to the question: 'How do I get further faster?'

Top three tips for creating successful partnerships

Doing it alone is no longer a viable option with the fast pace of change we are experiencing, and it is not slowing down, so you need to get on board. To keep up, we all need to work together.

If I have convinced you that collaboration is fundamental in the future of work regardless of where you are in your life journey, then here are my tips for creating successful partnerships that not only stand the test of time but lay the framework for you to achieve what we currently deem impossible.

1. FIT THE PIECES OF THE PUZZLE TOGETHER

As much as we would all love to work with people we fundamentally like, that defeats the purpose of true strategic partnership. Instead look at your personal goals and passion points like a puzzle that needs to fit together. View yourself as one puzzle piece. If you find someone who is similar to you in experience and skill set, unfortunately they are not adding any value to the overall puzzle. You will just have a bunch of similar puzzle pieces scattered on a board.

Assess both your own and your collaborator's skill sets. Do they complement each other? If so, how? It is not enough to depend solely on diversity. You need to be strategic in the alignment of that diversity. You need to think ahead in terms of how combining those diverse skill sets or experiences will help you achieve your goals.

Often people who are highly skilled in areas in which you are lacking tend to have quite different characteristics than you, which can put people off at the outset. But persevere to a place of greater understanding with your objectives in mind and it will be well worth it.

It is important to stress that assessing other people's skill sets should not be taken at face value. Just as Ja Rule heard through the grapevine that McFarland was a child prodigy and assumed his entrepreneurial flair would create a luxury-money-can't-buy festival experience out of thin air, do not make the same mistake by reading, rather than assessing, skill sets and ambitions. You need first-hand accounts and ideally an opportunity to work with the partner in question before cementing your collaboration. Remember, the aim is to create a true collaboration which becomes a long-term partnership, not a teaser campaign.

2. UNDERSTAND WHAT EACH PARTY BRINGS TO THE TABLE

Having a diverse set of skills to access as the project develops is critical for remaining competitive in a fast-moving environment, but each party should be explicit about what their individual objectives are. They should each have their own goals and know how their individual actions play into the wider objective. To do this you need clearly defined roles and responsibilities.

In addition, there need to be individual OKRs for each party so that development and advancement continue in each area, again employing the marginal gains theory. These individual OKRs are then measured against the overall OKR, ensuring all parties strive towards a single goal. This should be clearly laid out at the start to avoid redundant tasks, wasted time and gaps in execution.

3. TRUST

Building trust takes time, but is required in order to rely on others in any environment. The future of work is no different. Trust is paramount to ensure the actions everyone has agreed to will be executed as planned. Without trust, no partnership will be strong enough to withstand the hardships and challenges that inevitably come with building something truly remarkable.

Toothpaste isn't usually known for innovation...

It is predictable that I would promote partnerships as the way of the future considering I spent my career creating them. I have witnessed the enormous benefits from true collaboration, but I also know that partnerships can be hard work. This is why many leaders steer clear. With so many variables at play when two or more parties come together, you can never predict the outcome. This is vastly harder than working alone. When you only have yourself to blame, work can seem much easier to manage and often means you can be more agile at the beginning. But as I have discovered in over a decade creating some of the world's most successful partnerships, the power of collaboration far exceeds that of working in isolation.

My favourite example of the power of collaboration that demonstrates unseen potential is the McLaren Automotive Group's partnership with multinational pharmaceutical company GlaxoSmithKline (GSK), which came about through the Formula One race circuit. Often cited as a platform for traditional sponsorship deals where brands pay large sums of money to have their company logo placed on a Formula One car, the circuit has created one of the most exceptionally unique partnerships and illustrates how breaking some rules can create enormous success.

Formula One is known for the amount of data and technology required to operate automobiles at 200+ miles per hour around a race course, but not as well known for the people who analyse that data. But the data analysis behind a split-second decision can make the difference between winning or losing a race, or even the death of a driver. The data, computing and engineering required to run a successful Formula One team are astounding, a reality not lost on GSK, who cleverly realized they could have other applications.

GSK's Consumer Healthcare Division makes several different kinds of toothpaste under the brand names Sensodyne and Aquafresh. The productivity at these high-speed toothpaste manufacturing plants was suffering because of the large amount of downtime required to switch over the production lines from one type of toothpaste to the other, a similar plight of other manufacturers we saw earlier in the book. If GSK could reduce that downtime by half it would mean producing an additional 6.7 million tubes of toothpaste per year and revenue of $16.75 million.

With so much potential revenue lost each year, GSK searched far and wide for engineers who could solve this problem, but it was not until they approached Formula One team McLaren Automotive that they were finally able to solve it. Thinking outside the box, GSK offered to sponsor the team, but not in exchange for the typical logo on the side of the race car. Instead, GSK wanted access to the McLaren engineers in the off season.

Specifically, GSK asked McLaren's engineers to revamp their high-speed toothpaste lines. Using the same data-driven engineering techniques required to compete in Formula One, McLaren was able to reduce the line switchover time by 60 per cent, from 39 minutes down to 15 minutes.[26] A tremendous success making GSK millions.

This partnership propelled GSK beyond what they were achieving by themselves and could have only been achieved through collaboration. So successful, the two companies have rolled rolling out their proprietary high-speed engineering systems in factories around the world, setting a new standard for the manufacturing industry.

As this chapter has outlined, partnerships are the way of the future if you create them using the new rules for success. Although this is not always easy, it is necessary in the future of work because when all the puzzle pieces come together the opportunities are endless.

CHAPTER EIGHT

The future is here

Rule breakers will create change

We have arrived at the conclusion, which is in fact just the beginning of the journey. Although we may not be fully aware of it yet, we have each already started to forge new ways of working within the future of work. Whether it involves our desire to have a more flexible work–life balance or an instinctive need to create global change, we can all become rebel leaders in this context. The barriers are collapsing and we now have the potential to provide change for good. A change accelerated through the power of collaboration created with our new ability to tap into communities that exist beyond the regional boundaries that constrained us for thousands of years. The future of work is here, and we are all part of its interwoven fabric.

Throughout this book we have outlined the cause and effect of four decades of upheaval driven by the rise of the internet. We have witnessed the world wide web's launch into our lives for the purpose of tools. We actively supported its evolution and infiltration as it redefined our culture and purpose. As individuals, we have driven the radical use of addictive digital platforms fuelled by our desire for personal fulfilment. Collectively, we have seen the evolution of work failures and successes redefine our understanding of what is now possible with unicorn tech companies. It should be abundantly clear now that it is impossible for you to stand on the side-lines. Not because of urgency or necessity, but because our new world is so interconnected. Your action is as intrinsically linked to the world's outcome as your inaction. And for that reason, we must all choose to be active in order to participate in shaping the future. We are the future and the future is here.

But what does the future look like and how does the rebellious leadership approach we have laid out in these pages play into its evolution? To understand that in greater detail, let us examine the theory of our future from someone who already seems to have the crystal ball: US venture capitalist Bill Tai.

Along with funding start-ups with 22 IPOs, Tai is known for being one of the first investors in TweetDeck/Twitter. A man who proved his ability many times over in spotting a tech unicorn even before the term 'unicorn' was applied to the technology industry in 2013.[1] He has been a board director of eight publicly listed companies and his LinkedIn profile reads like a string of acronyms. Like many Silicon Valley leaders, he is as passionate about education as he is about kitesurfing and can often be found talking about the future at the World Economic Forum at Davos. Once quoted as 'the greatest venture capitalist to ever set foot on planet Earth', Tai is one man who never seems to get it wrong.[2] Which is probably why, in the decade I have known him, I have yet to see him frown.

As part of maintaining his competitive edge picking the businesses and leaders of the future, you would be surprised to find that his approach to success is much more relaxed than his venture capitalist counterparts. He is more at home identifying as a collaborator than a mystic fortune teller of billion-dollar market capitalizations. More likely to be found wearing board shorts on the beach than Savile Row tailored suits in the boardroom. This in itself is telling and hints at the secret to his success.

When I spoke to Tai about the future of work as it relates to business structures and future leadership, he highlighted the importance of people going back to basics. Rather than adjusting our caveman sensibilities to a new world with digital tools, we need instead to view digital tools as the opportunity to return to our caveman sensibilities. He argues that what makes us fundamentally human has not changed and the reason for so much discordance in the world today is this widening gap between our instincts and our actions due to the evolution of technology. However, we can change that by realigning ourselves with our values.

Tai argues that when our future is viewed in a wider context, the entirety of 6 million years of human evolution, the societal and business structures developed through the Industrial Revolution have only been in place for an incredibly small fraction of time. Even in comparison to the modern and organized civilization of 6,000 years, our recent drive for mass corporation building has only existed for 5 per cent of modern-day society. A small amount of time by any comparison.

We can trace this back to the First Industrial Revolution, which began in the mid-18th century, driven by our newly developed ability to use basic materials, mainly iron and steel, for production using steam. This created a new way of working known as the factory system, which prioritized division of labour. This was a miracle at the time and provided confidence in man's ability to master mother nature.

One hundred years later those methods gave way to the creation of synthetic resources and automation away from the assembly line, ushering in the age of mass production of the Second Industrial Revolution. Confidence grew further still as we developed changes in business ownership. As we outlined earlier with the Dutch East India Company, the creation of stocks allowed individuals and institutions to become equity owners, which opened a new wave of creation, ambition and drive for new frontiers.

Beginning in the 1950s the Third Industrial Revolution brought semiconductors, mainframe computing, personal computing and the internet. We outlined how this revolution created an unstable launch pad into our Fourth Industrial Revolution. Many would argue that we are standing on the edge of this leap; however, the case studies throughout this book suggest we are already well into the thick of it.

It is important to acknowledge the acceleration of change throughout these industrial revolutions, which by now should come as no surprise. Change is happening more quickly, and we need to be prepared. While adaptability is key, some of this preparation is about going back to basics. But change does not mean a complete reinvention of values. As Tai told me:

The future is actually the continuum humans have lived in for most of their existence. The relatively recent past of the last three generations which was made up of large corporations was a blip. A bubble. Not an indication of the future direction of societal structures. The ability to enslave humans as labour into boxes around a machine is a new structure. For the other 398,850 of 400,000 years people were fluid. What they worked on every day was fluid. For example, one might pick berries with five other people in the morning and then join six different people to fish for the rest of the day. Work was flexible and inspiration-based. That is the true nature of humans. It was interrupted for a brief moment by capital assets, but as we move to a fully digital economy, people are no longer tied to capital assets with false promises of lifelong pensions. They are now part of a flexible human fabric again. No one in the future will become a salary man because that was not real in the first place.[3]

This links back to defining our true purpose and driving that purpose through inspiration. That advancement, whether singularly or collectively, can be as simple as taking pleasure in the things we enjoy or as ambitious as saving the planet from destruction. The choice is ours. What is revolutionary is that we now have the tools at our disposal to work in the way we were always built to. A way in which, as Tai argues, we have always done before any industrial revolutions pushed us on the hamster wheel of mass production. We are evolving back to basics.

If we are going back to basics and inspiring people rather than chaining them to large capital-scale assets, then what lessons do we need to carry forward as we progress in the future of work collaboratively? For this we need a world of rebels. A generation of people not afraid to stand up for what they believe in and champion the issues they hold most dear. To rebel against the mass-produced assembly lines and back into a fully immersive digital economy with purpose at its core.

This is at odds with what we have been doing for the past 300 years. At odds with all the textbooks we have been studying and all the webinars we have been watching. Only by looking outside the box and breaking all the rules will we be able to progress in this new way of working.

Driving purpose through rebellious leadership

We have illustrated the importance of rebelliousness as core to the future of leadership, but it is important to recall that rebels are not necessarily pirates or aggressors. Not necessarily outliers of society. You will not find them wearing all black and discussing the future behind closed doors. Instead our future rebel leaders are active. They are sharing, they are collaborating and they are everywhere. They reflect the shifting structures of society: the future of work as we know it. They are rebelling against the generational patterns of business that have only existed for a moment in time and going back to instinct and fluidity. Productivity now comes from organizing a network of people who can be distributed rather than locked down in an assembly line and these rebels know how to make that happen. These are the leaders we have been waiting for.

Although the world has changed dramatically, the importance of achievement and communication has not. Those rebels going against the grain are not necessarily trying to radically disrupt the model, but instead moving us towards a better way of working. A way of working that has existed for millions of years. We have just not realized it until now. They are joining the front line with new tools to repave an old path based on new rules. Trends including flexible working and purpose-driven workplaces are arguably the core of what makes us human, and not a fad of the previous century.

The act of being more rebellious allows us to tap into what is already within us, breaking the shackles of centuries of work constraints that drove success for the few at the expense of the many. Success is now available to all through decentralization where the purpose is designed to be distributed. People are core to this flexibility. As we have witnessed with all the case studies in this book, this new way of leading works best when it is collaborative, open and transparent rather than closed and proprietary. Boundaries of success have been broken down by having more people included and joining in the evolution through contribution. This radical approach needs radical thinking and radical thinking needs a rebellious leader at its core.

So, if the goal is to go back to the basics of human fluidity where work is driven by the individual, then how does championing rebellious leadership support that endeavour?

As we have argued throughout the pages in this book, to become an effective leader in the future of work we must tap into our inner rebel rather than follow old rules. Old rules generated old methods of success and achievement. But as we have advanced beyond this, we need new rules. It takes bravery to follow them and forge our own paths.

Being known as a rebel, to defy the old way of doing things and lead from the front, is more in line with true leadership today. A leader who stands up for others and for themselves. A leader who is not afraid of stating what they believe in and even less afraid to take the steps necessary to put their beliefs into action. Gone are the days when leaders and organizations did not need to align to a purpose or a moral compass. In today's world, lacking either will result in becoming obsolete.

But standing up for what you believe in has consequences and not everyone likes the confrontation and criticism that can follow. Therefore, rousing your inner maverick is helpful to fighting the good fight. It is important to stop hesitating and instead view critiques as a way to engage and drive the conversation forward. As we outlined in Chapter 5, we need to welcome diverse thinking and embrace commentary. Any leader can withstand criticism (whether they like it or not), but a rebellious leader will view criticism as a driver of progress.

Beer mats for Brexit

Even in uncertain times, the value of standing for something is fundamental in the future of work. No one knows this more than the JD Wetherspoon chairman and founder Tim Martin.

British pub company JD Wetherspoon is an institution. It is almost impossible to visit London and not find yourself ducking into one for an afternoon pint or as shelter from the rain. Founded in 1979, it floated on the London Stock Exchange in October 1992 with just 44 pubs. By 2020 it was operating 900 pubs across Britain. With an annual turnover of $2 billion, it and sells more curries in the United Kingdom than any other restaurant in the country. In terms of footfall, in 2018 it was estimated over 17.4 million people had eaten in a Wetherspoon's pub in just six months, which is a reach of over 26 per cent of the total British population.[4] When assessing its influence over the drinking population it is significantly higher, making up 60 per cent.[5] One could argue that its reach and individual engagement make Wetherspoon more influential than the British media. A concept not lost on its founder.

In the months leading up to the EU referendum in 2016, politically engaged Martin took an active stance to get involved in the debate, using his pubs as a platform for his pro-Brexit campaign in the form of printed beer mats. Regardless of which side you stood, the country was divided and so taking any political viewpoint at all would seem illogical, detrimental even, to the pub's bottom line. It was a strong stance to take and although Martin still owned 32 per cent of the company, the remaining shares were held by investors on behalf of pension funds which are notoriously risk averse. Unsurprisingly, Martin's pro-Brexit beer mats were not supported by the stakeholders.

This controversial activity sparked a public outcry, with influential monitor of corporate governance Pirc publicly stating that 'the bulk of shareholders would want him to continue to focus on the business and to drop his personal views on Brexit'.[6] Shortly after that public statement was made, a further recommendation was made by Pirc to oppose Martin's re-election as chairman of the business at its 2019 annual general meeting. To increase pressure, shareholders and Pirc were quick to utilize the media. With visible external pressure so high, one can only imagine what kind of pressure Martin was experiencing internally. Despite it all, Martin did not back down. Regardless of where you stand on the issue of Brexit, what is interesting is that his act of defiance and his integrity won the respect of his customers and on 21 November 2019, 98 per cent of votes cast at the AGM were in favour of Martin's re-election.

Brexit was one of the most polarizing issues that ever faced the United Kingdom. For a business as prominent in the day-to-day lives as Wetherspoon to take a stance on such a divisive issue, whether you agree with it or not, while maintaining profits shows just how important having purpose is. People respect others who stand for something even if they might not agree.

Take a knee, others will follow

It can often be easier when you are a business founder to take a stance, but that does not mean that you should not stand for something if you work within an organization. Often times it is taking action internally which can inspire a movement, as professional American football player Colin Kaepernick has proven.

Kaepernick sparked international discourse when he began kneeling during the national anthem before games to protest racism, social inequality and police brutality following a wave of shootings of unarmed African–American men by the police in August 2016. His actions were soon followed by players from other teams and even athletes in other sports joined Kaepernick in kneeling, locking arms or raising fists in support of his message. But his peaceful protest was not supported by NFL executives and even drew vocal criticism from former President Trump who called for protesting players to be fired.[7] Following Kaepernick's departure from the San Francisco 49ers at the end of the season to become a free agent, no other team signed him.

At the time it seemed like standing for something meant he had to lose his dream of playing professional football. He was all alone. An outcast of the NFL. Fortunately, his bravery did not go unnoticed. While many brands would have dropped endorsement deals with the football star purely because he was no longer on the field and therefore would not be able to provide exposure, Nike did the opposite and doubled down. In an unprecedented move they chose to help Kaepernick amplify his message, making him the focus of their 30th anniversary 'Just do it' campaign. The campaign was bold and featured the quarterback with the slogan 'Believe in something. Even if it means sacrificing everything'.

It was a contentious move, the ad campaign initially sparking protests among some consumers and causing Nike's share price to fall by 2 per cent. Responses ranged from people burning trainers to boycotting the brand, hitting out on Twitter using the hashtag #JustBurnIt which trended alongside #BoycottNike. But it did not take long for the brand to rebound, with Nike stock closing at $119 in September 2020, an all-time high for the apparel maker. Proof that standing for something in the future of work despite criticism or pressure is the only way to become a true leader. It might take time, but by taking a stance and using your voice, others who are aligned will follow. A concept not lost on Nike founder Phil Knight who stated:

> It doesn't matter how many people hate your brand as long as enough people love it. As long as you have that attitude, you can't be afraid of offending people. You can't try and go down the middle of the road. You have to take a stand on something, which is ultimately I think why the Kaepernick ad worked.[8]

Four years after Kaepernick's protest, professional sports teams and athletes started to follow suit, supporting the Black Lives Matter movement by boycotting play in August 2020. Major League Baseball, Major League Soccer, National Hockey League, the National Basketball Association and the Women's National Basketball Association all postponed games, some even playoff games, in their efforts towards social justice.

So when your confidence falters or criticism keeps you up at night, remember that purpose is now what drives the future, even if that future is not immediate. By tapping into your inner rebel you can find the courage to lead that purpose through challenging times when pressure mounts. It is only then that you will be victorious in your mission and empower change to happen.

Collaboration and shared ownership

As we have seen throughout this book, leadership is no longer a singular pursuit to climb the ivory tower and dictate to those below. The future of leadership is about inspiring and organizing others around purpose. In that sense it can be difficult to identify true rebellious leaders, mainly because they rarely identify themselves as such. Instead modern rebellious leaders see themselves as collaborators.

Remember Kylie Jenner? Her meteoric rise from a modern-day socialite to a beauty tycoon happened organically, if not propelled by the media platform from which she built her following. Capitalizing through instinct and authenticity, not strategically masterminded by big business, her influence has been developed through her execution. Jenner has made waves not because of her selfies but by paving a new path for doing business by navigating networks and understanding the value of strategic partnerships.

Since the launch of her infamous lip kits, brands have started to take notice and push the boundaries beyond the assembly-line structures of the beauty industry's past. Accelerated by the lack of authenticity seen in the age of influencers, purpose and collaboration are being utilized in functions that were not possible even a couple of years ago. What makes the next decade truly revolutionary is that we are building on the successes and lessons learned, evolving into a business model where everyone benefits.

The gig economy laid the groundwork. But after witnessing the ravages of business rather than taking advantage and pushing margins, the newly evolved gig economy is progressing into one of shared ownership and shared contribution. A concept that is starting to become central to new business functions of the future.

Sharing is caring

MyBeautyBrand is one such company evolving the gig economy to the benefit of all its partners. Rather than succumbing to the click-bait world of social media influence, the digital peer-to-peer platform MyBeautyBrand provides shared ownership. It is a platform that allows individuals to not only create make-up looks but also share in the profits by tagging products and earning commission on sales. Unlike Kylie Cosmetics, which follows beauty trends and quickly turns them into products for purchase, MyBeautyBrand empowers young beauty creatives to focus on their individual craft rather than spending time chasing social media followers to sell to. It is beauty for the people, by the people. It is as authentic as it comes in the beauty industry and a strong stance against the beauty influencers and bloggers that initially proliferated the new beauty scene. In fact, the MyBeautyBrand founders set it up as a reaction to the industry's pervasive influencer culture.

As co-founder Robin Derrick puts it: 'People forget that the original blogger culture existed to call journalists out. It was the voice of the people and very much against journalists regurgitating press releases. It was very anti-journalism'. Derrick is clear about his own motivation to launch MyBeautyBrand, stating that it was his reaction to the onslaught of influencers. He wanted to go back to basics and create a company that was more authentic, 'just a girl in her bedroom who was a part-time writer'.[9]

It is this authenticity that resonates throughout the entire business with a manifesto so bold it is printed on their T-shirts in order to help spread the message. The language is rousing and inclusive: 'I'm sick of the braggers, the blaggers and the hashtaggers. Sick of the takers and the 'no-filter' fakers. I'm sick of the fads. I'm sick of the ads and the wouldn't be famous if it wasn't for your dads...' reinforcing the influencer fatigue so many are feeling.[10]

Predictably the first MyBeautyBrand store owners were students, earning shares to help pay for their tuition at the famous art college Central Saint Martins in London, where Derrick teaches. This only adds to the appeal. With commission of up to 20 per cent of sales, it is a platform that doesn't just promote authenticity, it rewards it. An organization that is about the community it serves as much as it is for the contributors it works with. An organization that will grow with its community rather than profit from it. This is not just the future of beauty. This is the future of business. Where everyone involved benefits and where positive change happens.

You are the future

Although he might not recognize it, my first employee Mark Mylam exemplifies a future leader. It is why I hired him eight years ago. Interestingly, Mark has used many of the tools of this book to his advantage and broken some rules along the way. Most notable was his decision to give up his place at law school to pursue a career in sports marketing and come and work for me. I imagine when he gave up his place he did not expect to work in a shoe closet, but as he puts it: 'It was the best decision I ever made.' He remembers being horrified by the stories from friends of working past midnight on a daily basis and sleeping under desks, friends who worked at law firms he initially aspired to work for. In the end, he chose to follow passion over a pay-cheque.

This comes as no surprise. But noteworthy is how such a seemingly minor decision is generating a major shift in the global consciousness of future leaders. The decision to ditch law school changed everything for Mark and along the way has shaped his view of the world. But Mark's experience reflects an *entire generation* of people who have made similar career decisions.

With this comes a new generation who have completely new values, bringing a significant cultural change in leadership. People are making different choices, which are radically changing the course of history. No longer motivated purely by money, people are driven by their passion. This book has outlined the people and businesses already leading in this way, which explains their remarkable success. These examples illustrate how breaking rules will lead to positive change. Something we are all in need of.

I initially spoke with Mark back in 2019 when I proposed including him in this book. I recall that evening sitting around my kitchen table talking politics and drinking wine, not worrying about hand sanitizer or being socially distanced. It seems like a million years ago. Things have changed so much.

Most apparent was the seismic shift to remote working. Although this had been debated for many years, the pandemic forced many businesses to make working from home work for them. Post-pandemic remote working will become standard, which creates countless new opportunities for workers. This new norm was famously spearheaded by Twitter which announced in May 2020 that all employees could work from home 'forever'. Shortly after, Shopify announced they were closing their offices until 2021 to 'rework them for this new reality'.[11]

But it is not just big tech giants that are reconsidering their business model post-pandemic. Even traditional organizations are changing the way they do things. A study by KPMG surveyed 1,300 large company CEOs before the impacts of the lockdown were felt, then followed this up with a further survey in the summer of 2020. The results showed a significant change in priorities in that short timeframe between the two surveys. Specifically, the study reported that many businesses' attitudes are evolving quite significantly, and CEOs are starting to lead with increased purpose and impact, both societal and economic. In addition, more than two-thirds (69 per cent) were planning to downsize their office space and 79 per cent were re-evaluating their purpose as a result of the pandemic.[12]

With so much change in the wake of so much catastrophe, I wonder, have things changed for Mark? Now in his thirties, he is at a point in his life where the bigger life decisions need to be made. Where to live, where to work, who to work for and what to do. I imagine being stuck at home makes the weight of those decisions seem that much greater. Connecting on Zoom, he reflected on how much change he has encountered.[13] Mark told me:

> In the last six months my world has changed dramatically because of Covid-19.
>
> Isolation has forced me, like so many others, to take the time to reflect on what I want to do with the rest of my life. Although it has been a challenge, ironically it has also accelerated my desire to live a more fulfilled life and provided me with new opportunities to advance myself in ways I could not have done before.
>
> I think the world is finally waking up to the fact that the things that matter in life cannot be compartmentalized away from the work you do. It is this interconnectedness between personal values and work that no longer can be overlooked by leadership. Because of this, I think the future will look vastly different than it does today.
>
> Personally, I cannot wait.

Spoken like a true future leader.

ACKNOWLEDGEMENTS

We are living in crazy times. I am amazed at how much change is happening and although the themes of this book have been percolating in my brain for many years, I believe it has all come to a tipping point. For that, I am grateful to be able to write this book at such a pivotal moment in history.

I have been inspired by all the leaders who are not afraid to make change, not afraid to speak their minds. All the rebels who will not accept old rules and the mavericks who are redefining limitations. This book is for all of you.

I am also extremely grateful to everyone who contributed their time with interviews, feedback, discussions and inspiration: Mark Mylam, Maryam and Amina Mamilova, Bill Tai, Cory Johnson, Fahad Saud, Matthew d'Ancona, Rebecca Jolly, Elty Dudley-Williams, Cory Johnson, James Watt, Jamie Dey and Katie Cavanagh.

A big thank you to fellow rule breaker and my commissioning editor Géraldine Collard who made this all happen. This book would never have been written if you had not reached out.

Thanks especially to both sets of Hendrix's grandparents: Shirley and Herman Fast and Sue and Roy Huston, without whose babysitting hours the completion of this book would not have been possible.

And finally, a big thank you to my husband Chris who not only inspired the best chapter in this book but continues to inspire me each and every day.

References

Chapter 1

1. Kuncel, NR, Ones, DS, Klieger, DM (2014) In hiring, algorithms beat instinct, *Harvard Business Review*, 1 May, hbr.org/2014/05/in-hiring-algorithms-beat-instinct (archived at https://perma.cc/2SJM-6G7T)
2. Worldometers (2020) World population online, www.worldometers.info/world-population/ (archived at https://perma.cc/YR5L-PHYT)
3. Robbins, T (2020) *Unleash the Power Within*, www.tonyrobbins.com/events/unleash-the-power-within/ (archived at https://perma.cc/HHU4-XNL8)
4. Robbins, T (2020) *Unleash the Power Within*, www.tonyrobbins.com/events/unleash-the-power-within/ (archived at https://perma.cc/HHU4-XNL8)
5. NCCA Research, Estimated probability of Competing in Athletics Beyond the High School Interscholastic Level, https://www.wiaawi.org/Portals/0/PDF/Publications/probabilitybeyondhs.pdf (archived at https://perma.cc/J5MR-YDDP)
6. Petram, LO (2011) *The World's First Stock Exchange: How the Amsterdam market for Dutch East India Company shares became a modern securities market, 1602–1700*, Eigen Beheer
7. Taylor, B (2013) The rise and fall of the largest corporation in history, *Business Insider*, 6 November, www.businessinsider.com/rise-and-fall-of-united-east-india-2013-11?r=US&IR=T (archived at https://perma.cc/DSG2-YU3N)
8. Slater, M (2012) Olympics cycling: Marginal gains underpin Team GB dominance, BBC Sport, 8 August, www.bbc.co.uk/sport/olympics/19174302 (archived at https://perma.cc/NNJ2-7S7K)
9. Hoogveld, M (2017) *Agile Management: The fast and flexible approach to continuous improvement and innovation in organizations*, Business Expert Press, New York
10. Clear, J (2018) *Atomic Habits: An easy and proven way to build good habits and break bad ones*, Random House USA, New York

11. Scott Pelley, Howard Schultz: The Star Of Starbucks, *60 Minutes/CBS News*, https://www.cbsnews.com/news/howard-schultz-the-star-of-starbucks/ (archived at https://perma.cc/P9H9-9PE5)

12. World Airline Awards (2019) World's Top 100 Airlines 2019, www.worldairlineawards.com/worlds-top-100-airlines-2019/ (archived at https://perma.cc/Q4LV-NLXQ)

13. Allende, S (2018) *Be More Pirate: Or how to take on the world and win*, Touchstone, New York

Chapter 2

1. Daily Mail Reporter (2006) Sir Richard Branson: Me and my money, Thisismoney, 19 July, www.thisismoney.co.uk/money/meandmymoney/article-1600580/Sir-Richard-Branson-Me-money.html (archived at https://perma.cc/Z5K4-S54L)

2. Fagone, J (2013) *Ingenious: A true story of invention, automotive daring, and the race to revive America*, Crown, New York

3. Melton, J (2018) E-commerce has an outsized impact on the CPG market, research shows, DigitalCommerce360, 18 October, www.digitalcommerce360.com/2018/10/18/e-commerce-has-an-outsized-impact-on-the-fmcg-market-research-shows/ (archived at https://perma.cc/49BX-W3NF)

4. CSPonline (2016) *From Storefronts to Search Engines: A history of e-commerce*, Concordia St. Paul, 28 July, online.csp.edu/blog/business/history-of-ecommerce/ (archived at https://perma.cc/C4WH-3ENK)

5. Biron, B (2019) Beauty has blown up to be a $532 billion industry – and analysts say that these 4 trends will make it even bigger, *Business Insider*, www.businessinsider.com/beauty-multibillion-industry-trends-future-2019-7?r=US&IR=T (archived at https://perma.cc/856V-BWQR)

6. Robehmed, N (2019) How Rihanna Created A $600 Million Fortune—And Became The World's Richest Female Musician, *Forbes*, https://www.forbes.com/sites/natalierobehmed/2019/06/04/rihanna-worth-fenty-beauty/?sh=2c1f0efa13de (archived at https://perma.cc/8FDF-2VXK)

7. L'Oréal Finance (2019) 2018 Annual Results: Best sales growth in more than 10 years: +7.1%, New record for operating margin: 18.3%, L'Oréal Finance, 7 February, www.loreal-finance.com/eng/news-release/2018-annual-results (archived at https://perma.cc/BY7E-3C9U)

8. Schiffer, J (2018) The secret company behind KKW Beauty and Kylie Cosmetics, InStyle, 20 July, www.instyle.com/news/secret-company-behind-kkw-beauty-and-kylie-cosmetics (archived at https://perma.cc/X3WQ-SLDG)

9. Robehmed, N (2018) How 20-Year-Old Kylie Jenner Built A $900 Million Fortune In Less Than 3 Years, Forbes, https://www.forbes.com/sites/forbesdigitalcovers/2018/07/11/how-20-year-old-kylie-jenner-built-a-900-million-fortune-in-less-than-3-years/?sh=2bc508bdaa62 (archived at https://perma.cc/8BD3-TM67)

10. Warren, K and Borden, T (2020) Kylie Jenner just turned 23 years old – and she's already worth $900 million. Take a look at how the mogul built her empire, Business Insider, https://www.businessinsider.com/how-does-kylie-jenner-make-money-2018-7?r=US&IR=T (archived at https://perma.cc/VYW2-9S8Q)

11. Naughton, J (2010) The internet: is it changing the way we think?, The Observer, 14 August, www.theguardian.com/technology/2010/aug/15/internet-brain-neuroscience-debate (archived at https://perma.cc/YD6C-CYUY)

12. Shane, D (2020) 96 percent of consumers don't trust ads. Here's how to sell your product without coming off sleazy, Inc.com, 6 October, www.inc.com/dakota-shane/96-percent-of-consumers-dont-trust-ads-heres-how-to-sell-your-product-without-coming-off-sleazy.html (archived at https://perma.cc/QKQ9-R8NH)

13. Garvin, R (2019) How social networks influence 74% of shoppers for their purchasing decisions today, Awario.com, 11 May, awario.com/blog/how-social-networks-influence-74-of-shoppers-for-their-purchasing-decisions-today/ (archived at https://perma.cc/2J8J-7ADL)

14. Warren, K and Borden, T (2020) Kylie Jenner just turned 23 years old – and she's already worth $900 million. Take a look at how the mogul built her empire, Business Insider, 10 August, www.businessinsider.com/how-does-kylie-jenner-make-money-2018-7?r=US&IR=T#:~:text=In%20March%202019%2C%20Forbes%20dubbed,than%20%20241%20billion%2C%20Forbes%20said (archived at https://perma.cc/YSW5-LNXE)

15. Weiner, Z (2018) Kylie Jenner opens up about her lip injections and starting Kylie Cosmetics, TeenVogue.com, 2 May, www.teenvogue.com/story/kylie-jenner-lip-insecurity-kylie-cosmetics (archived at https://perma.cc/Q384-CXLW)

16. Hendricks, D (2013) The complete history of social media: Then and now, Smallbiztrends.com, 8 May, smallbiztrends.com/2013/05/the-complete-history-of-social-media-infographic.html#:~:text= The%20first%20recognizable%20social%20media,sensation%20 that's%20still%20popular%20today (archived at https://perma.cc/QUZ3-QL3E)

17. Allam, R (2017) Forbes Rolls Out First Top Influencer List, *About Her*, https://www.abouther.com/node/2231/people/influencers/forbes-rolls-out-first-top-influencer-list (archived at https://perma.cc/FSS4-YQ3D)

18. Schomer, A (2019) Influencer marketing: State of the social media influencer market in 2020, *Business Insider*, 17 December, www.businessinsider.com/influencer-marketing-report?r=US&IR=T (archived at https://perma.cc/324V-KL6G)

19. Patel, S (2017) Inside Disney's troubled $675 mil. Maker Studios acquisition, Digiday.com, 22 February, digiday.com/future-of-tv/disney-maker-studios/ (archived at https://perma.cc/LX56-RPS3)

20. Interview with M.92

21. Bramley, EV (2020) Makeover: Copenhagen fashion week announces 'radical' sustainability goals, *The Guardian*, 29 January, www.theguardian.com/fashion/2020/jan/29/make-over-copenhagen-fashion-week-announces-radical-sustainability-goals (archived at https://perma.cc/5T7M-SRKV)

22. Fitzgerald, M (2020) Rapid CEO turnover continues with a record number of top executives departing in January, CNBC, 12 February, www.cnbc.com/2020/02/12/rapid-ceo-turnover-continues-with-a-record-number-of-top-executives-departing-in-january.html (archived at https://perma.cc/SXF7-F337)

Chapter 3

1. Imagining the internet, Elon University, online, www.elon.edu/u/imagining/expert_predictions/being-digital-a-book-preview-3/ (archived at https://perma.cc/RZ9Y-JSAD)

2. Frauenfelder, M (2019) Stewart Brand talks about the LSD trip that inspired his Whole Earth Catalog, Boingboing.net, 8 April, boingboing.net/2019/04/08/stewart-brand-talks-about-the.html (archived at https://perma.cc/8FSA-U33T)

3. Kabil, A (2018) Seeing the whole Earth from space changed everything, Medium.com, 15 May, medium.com/the-long-now-foundation/earth-and-civilization-in-the-macroscope-82243cad20bd (archived at https://perma.cc/B8ER-SREE)

4. Kabil, A (2018) Seeing the whole Earth from space changed everything, Medium.com, 15 May, medium.com/the-long-now-foundation/earth-and-civilization-in-the-macroscope-82243cad20bd (archived at https://perma.cc/B8ER-SREE)

5. History.com (2010) *The Space Race*, A&E Television Networks, 22 February, www.history.com/topics/cold-war/space-race (archived at https://perma.cc/JT7Q-P6AG)

6. Cadwalladr, C (2013) Stewart Brand's Whole Earth Catalog: The book that changed the world, *The Observer*, 5 May, www.theguardian.com/books/2013/may/05/stewart-brand-whole-earth-catalog (archived at https://perma.cc/JYZ6-TVEG)

7. Cadwalladr, C (2013) Stewart Brand's Whole Earth Catalog, the book that changed the world, *The Guardian*, https://www.theguardian.com/books/2013/may/05/stewart-brand-whole-earth-catalog (archived at https://perma.cc/EB7G-RUDE)

8. Cadwalladr, C (2013) Stewart Brand's Whole Earth Catalog: The book that changed the world, *The Observer*, 5 May, www.theguardian.com/books/2013/may/05/stewart-brand-whole-earth-catalog (archived at https://perma.cc/JYZ6-TVEG)

9. Daily FT (2017) Post-truth is Oxford Dictionaries Word of the Year, 4 February, www.ft.lk/front-page/post-truth-is-oxford-dictionaries-word-of-the-year/44-595865 (archived at https://perma.cc/Z3XG-VMJQ)

10. Egan, T (2016) The post-truth presidency, *The New York Times*, 4 November, www.nytimes.com/2016/11/04/opinion/campaign-stops/the-post-truth-presidency.html (archived at https://perma.cc/2BHK-2YNS)

11. Hotten, R (2015) Volkswagen: The scandal explained, *BBC News*, https://www.bbc.co.uk/news/business-34324772 (archived at https://perma.cc/2BHK-2YNS)

12. Yates, SQ (2016) Deputy Attorney General Sally Q Yates delivers remarks at press conference announcing $14.7 billion Volkswagen settlements, press release, 28 June, www.justice.gov/opa/speech/deputy-attorney-general-sally-q-yates-delivers-remarks-press-conference-announcing-147 (archived at https://perma.cc/XX8X-6U6B)

13. d'Ancona, M (2017) *Post-truth: the new war on truth and how to fight back*, Ebury Press, London

14. Interview with Matthew d'Ancona

15. *New York Times* (2018) New York primary election results, *The New York Times*, 28 June, www.nytimes.com/interactive/2018/06/26/us/elections/results-new-york-primary-elections.html?mtrref=undefined&gwh=18F93403596BC70169896AD9D287D04A&gwt=pay&assetType=REGIWALL (archived at https://perma.cc/U4AJ-ELSK)

16. Chavez, A and Grim, R (2018) A primary against the machine: A Bronx activist looks to dethrone Joseph Crowley, the King of Queens, The Intercept, 22 May, theintercept.com/2018/05/22/joseph-crowley-alexandra-ocasio-cortez-new-york-primary/ (archived at https://perma.cc/KM3G-BM4X)

17. D'Onfro, J (2019) Google's Approval Of $135 Million Payout To Execs Accused Of Sexual Misconduct Sparks Fresh Employee Backlash, *Forbes*, https://www.forbes.com/sites/jilliandonfro/2019/03/12/googles-approval-of-135-million-payout-to-execs-accused-of-sexual-misconduct-sparks-fresh-employee-backlash/?sh=6b4e3fcb3cf3 (archived at https://perma.cc/4FJV-VCAH)

18. Amazon Employees for Climate Justice (2019) Open letter to Jeff Bezos and the Amazon Board of Directors, Medium.com, 10 April, medium.com/@amazonemployeesclimatejustice/public-letter-to-jeff-bezos-and-the-amazon-board-of-directors-82a8405f5e38 (archived at https://perma.cc/FUH5-8D92)

19. Amazon Employees for Climate Justice (2019) @AMZNforClimate [Twitter], medium.com/@amazonemployeesclimatejustice/public-letter-to-jeff-bezos-and-the-amazon-board-of-directors-82a8405f5e38 (archived at https://perma.cc/FUH5-8D92)

20. Bezos, J (2020) Today, I'm thrilled to announce I am launching the Bezos Earth Fund, Instagram, 11 February, www.instagram.com/p/B8rWKFnnQ5c/?utm_source=ig_embed (archived at https://perma.cc/U43V-F6TP)

21. Petrov, C (2020) 21+ freelance statistics to know in May 2020, Spendmenot.com, 24 June, spendmenot.com/blog/freelance-statistics/ (archived at https://perma.cc/RD7V-FVNH)

22. Goodkind, N (2019) New Jersey exemplifies the long, confusing road ahead to legislate the gig economy, Fortune.com, 3 December, fortune.com/2019/12/03/ab5-law-gig-economy-california-new-jersey/ (archived at https://perma.cc/ZM3K-8G9D)

23. McCue, TJ (2018) 57 million US workers are part of the gig economy, *Forbes*, 31 August, www.forbes.com/sites/tjmccue/2018/08/31/57-million-u-s-workers-are-part-of-the-gig-economy/#6a9d0ed17118 (archived at https://perma.cc/ZN6J-45SC)

24. Partington, R (2019) Gig economy in Britain doubles, accounting for 4.7 million workers, *The Guardian*, 28 June, www.theguardian.com/business/2019/jun/28/gig-economy-in-britain-doubles-accounting-for-47-million-workers (archived at https://perma.cc/EV8M-FFB2)

25. WBUR (2018) The origin story of the gig economy [podcast,] 20 August, www.wbur.org/onpoint/2018/08/20/gig-economy-temp-louis-hyman (archived at https://perma.cc/H9HZ-S38P)

26. Overfelt, M (2017) The new generation of employees would take less pay for these job perks, CNBC.com, 31 May, www.cnbc.com/2017/05/30/job-perks-prodding-millennials-to-work-for-less.html (archived at https://perma.cc/STF2-AW9M)

27. Le Meur, L (2015) The smartest people in the world don't work for you, Medium.com, 27 October, medium.com/swlh/the-smartest-people-in-the-world-don-t-work-for-you-46d7b69eb65d (archived at https://perma.cc/Q5YQ-HKW7)

28. Wikipedia (2020) Joy's law (management), 12 September, en.wikipedia.org/wiki/Joy%27s_law_(management) (archived at https://perma.cc/KV5T-C7JM)

29. Bruce Daisley @brucedaisley [Twitter], twitter.com/brucedaisley?lang=en (archived at https://perma.cc/VVR5-58WS)

30. EatSleepWorkRepeat (2019) Modern work is a lie – Bruce Daisley [podcast, online video] www.youtube.com/watch?v=diSBPUs0t0Y&feature=youtu.be (archived at https://perma.cc/64MU-K9F2)

31. Deloitte (2019) *The Deloitte Global Millennial Survey 2019*, https://www2.deloitte.com/content/dam/Deloitte/global/Documents/About-Deloitte/deloitte-2019-millennial-survey.pdf (archived at https://perma.cc/UR4K-UZY9)

32. Fidelity Investments (2016) Better quality of work life is worth a $7,600 pay cut for millennials, Businesswire.com, 7 April, www.businesswire.com/news/home/20160407005736/en/Quality-Work-Life-Worth-7600-Pay-Cut (archived at https://perma.cc/ZM4S-5YDB)

33. McQueen, N (2018) Workplace culture trends: The key to hiring (and keeping) top talent in 2018, LinkedIn, 26 June, blog.linkedin.com/2018/june/26/workplace-culture-trends-the-key-to-hiring-and-keeping-top-talent (archived at https://perma.cc/6LTJ-RQUY)

34. Sinek, S (2011) *Start With Why: How Great Leaders Inspire Everyone To Take Action*, Porfolio, New York

35. WMFC (2017) Generational differences chart, www.wmfc.org/uploads/GenerationalDifferencesChart.pdf (archived at https://perma.cc/DH6T-7N6E)

Chapter 4

1. Young, A (2013) BrewDog caught up in ASA tussle, *The Drinks Business*, https://www.thedrinksbusiness.com/2013/07/brewdog-caught-up-in-asa-tussle/ (archived at https://perma.cc/R7WQ-C3Z7)

2. BrewDog (nd) Our Manifesto, https://www.brewdog.com/uk/community/culture/our-manifesto (archived at https://perma.cc/BMX9-K6BP)

3. Stoller, K (2020) The new beer barons: How two Scottish kids turned wild flavors, crowdfunding and plenty of attitude into a $2 billion business, *Forbes*, 14 January, www.forbes.com/sites/kristinstoller/2020/01/14/the-new-beer-barons-how-two-scottish-kids-turned-wild-flavors-crowdfunding-and-plenty-of-attitude-into-a-2-billion-business/#f87999829c4b (archived at https://perma.cc/8ZPE-LT9T)

4. BrewDog (2010) Why we do what we do, Brewdog.com (archived at https://perma.cc/7PK2-Y3SR), 21 June, www.brewdog.com/blog/why-we-do-what-we-do (archived at https://perma.cc/62YK-BQQF)

5. Wikipedia (2020) BrewDog, 25 August, en.wikipedia.org/wiki/BrewDog#cite_note-55 (archived at https://perma.cc/S2QV-RYM3)

6. Watt, J (2015) *Business for Punks: Break all the rules – The BrewDog way*, Portfolio Penguin, London

7. Wikipedia (2020) Mentorship, 11 October, en.wikipedia.org/wiki/
   Mentorship (archived at https://perma.cc/M8ZK-5FBR)

8. Zachary, L and Fishler, L (2009) *The Mentee's Guide: Making
   mentoring work for you*, Jossey-Bass, San Francisco

9. Phillips-Jones, L (2000), *The Mentee's Guide: How to have a
   successful relationship with a mentor*, Coalition of Counseling
   Centers, California

10. Shea, G (1999) *Making the Most of Being Mentored: How to grow
    from a mentoring partnership*, Crisp Publications, Menlo Park

11. Van Diggelen, A (2013) Elon Musk: On critics, Steve Jobs and
    innovation (transcript), freshdialogues.com, 25 February,
    www.freshdialogues.com/2013/02/25/elon-musk-on-steve-jobs-
    innovation-critics-transcript/ (archived at https://perma.cc/46DR-B2SE)

12. Economy, P (2019) The (Millennial) workplace of the future is almost
    here – these 3 things are about to change big time, Inc.com, 15 January,
    www.inc.com/peter-economy/the-millennial-workplace-of-future-is-
    almost-here-these-3-things-are-about-to-change-big-time.html
    (archived at https://perma.cc/SMD4-NT7S)

13. AMEX (2017) Redefining the C-suite: Business the millennial way,
    www.americanexpress.com/content/dam/amex/uk/staticassets/pdf/
    AmexBusinesstheMillennialWay.pdf (archived at https://perma.cc/
    TWS2-DKX5)

14. Festinger, L (1962) Cognitive dissonance, *Scientific American*,
    October, www.scientificamerican.com/article/cognitive-dissonance/
    (archived at https://perma.cc/F2SR-QA8R)

15. Loose, T (2017) 10 best and worst jobs for work-life balance,
    HuffPost, 6 December, www.huffpost.com/entry/10-best-and-worst-
    jobs-fo_b_8924278?guccounter=1 (archived at https://perma.cc/
    K65H-R5DV)

16. Interview with Cory Johnson

17. Demers, J (2020) How much time do your employees waste at work
    each day?, Inc.com, 6 October, www.inc.com/jayson-demers/
    how-much-time-do-your-employees-waste-at-work-each-day.html
    (archived at https://perma.cc/9W4D-CE86)

18. Equality and Human Rights Commission (2017) The Disability Pay
    Gap, www.equalityhumanrights.com/sites/default/files/research-
    report-107-the-disability-pay-gap.pdf (archived at https://perma.cc/
    MN6V-RG98)

19. Ryan, F (2018) We know about the gender pay gap. But what about the disability pay gap? *The Guardian*, 11 April, www.theguardian.com/commentisfree/2018/apr/11/gender-pay-gap-disability-disabled-people-job (archived at https://perma.cc/PV9C-9PH9)

20. Hewlett, SA, Marshall M and Sherbin, L (2013) How diversity can drive innovation, *Harvard Business Review*, 1 December, hbr.org/2013/12/how-diversity-can-drive-innovation (archived at https://perma.cc/74PZ-3EQV)

21. Hastwell, C (2019) Millennials, Gen Xers and Boomers want different things from leaders, Greatplacetowork.com, 6 September. www.greatplacetowork.com/resources/blog/millennials-gen-xers-and-boomers-want-different-things-from-leaders (archived at https://perma.cc/PAC5-NULM)

22. Hastwell, C (2019) Millennials, Gen Xers and Boomers want different things from leaders, Greatplacetowork.com, 6 September, www.greatplacetowork.com/resources/blog/millennials-gen-xers-and-boomers-want-different-things-from-leaders (archived at https://perma.cc/PAC5-NULM)

23. Interview with Fahad Saud

24. Sloane, G (2017) Sean Parker says Facebook was designed to be addictive, Adage.com, 9 November, adage.com/article/digital/sean-parker-worries-facebook-rotting-children-s-brains/311238 (archived at https://perma.cc/Y79E-Z2P5)

25. Hosie, R (2018) Young people feel lonelier than any other age group, largest study into loneliness reveals, *The Independent*, 1 October, www.independent.co.uk/life-style/young-people-loneliness-intense-study-a8563056.html (archived at https://perma.cc/WT6Z-AY7M)

26. Konnikova, M (2014) The limits of friendship, *The New Yorker*, online, 7 October, www.newyorker.com/science/maria-konnikova/social-media-affect-math-dunbar-number-friendships (archived at https://perma.cc/QD37-RN4A)

27. Abbott, B (2019) Youth suicide rate increased 56% in decade, CDC Says, *The Wall Street Journal*, 17 October, www.wsj.com/articles/youth-suicide-rate-rises-56-in-decade-cdc-says-11571284861 (archived at https://perma.cc/7XKQ-HR3V)

28. McGee, C (2017) Only 4% of Uber drivers remain on the platform a year later, says report, CNBC, 20 April, www.cnbc.com/2017/04/20/

only-4-percent-of-uber-drivers-remain-after-a-year-says-report.html (archived at https://perma.cc/49AU-XNVR)

29. Sainato, M (2019) 'I made $3.75 an hour': Lyft and Uber drivers push to unionize for better pay, *The Guardian*, 22 March, www.theguardian.com/us-news/2019/mar/22/uber-lyft-ipo-drivers-unionize-low-pay-expenses (archived at https://perma.cc/MS2G-KF99)

30. Gurdus, L (2019) Uber stumbles in most-watched IPO since Facebook – Cramer and other experts on what's next, CNBC.com 10 May, www.cnbc.com/2019/05/10/uber-stumbles-in-ipocramer-and-other-experts-on-what-to-expect.html (archived at https://perma.cc/8BMZ-ZVNN)

31. Pietsch, B (2020) WeWork's valuation has fallen from $47 billion last year to $2.9 billion, *Business Insider*, 18 May, www.businessinsider.com/wework-valuation-falls-47-billion-to-less-than-3-billion-2020-5?r=US&IR=T (archived at https://perma.cc/PMG7-B7KY)

32. White, T (2020) Finally Fresh: Beers with James Watt of BrewDog, Hopculture.com, www.hopculture.com/the-hop-review/james-watt-brewdog/ (archived at https://perma.cc/MV25-MZED)

Chapter 5

1. McGrady, V (2015) 7 pro tips to help your home sell faster, for more money, *Forbes*, 4 November, www.forbes.com/sites/vanessamcgrady/2015/11/04/staging/#6b684d3150c9 (archived at https://perma.cc/B4ZC-A5W4)

2. Angeladuckworth.com [website] angeladuckworth.com/qa/ (archived at https://perma.cc/F523-QVYY)

3. Groth, A (2012) Malcolm Gladwell explains why underdogs win an 'astonishing' amount of the time, *Business Insider*, 9 July, www.businessinsider.com/malcolm-gladwell-explains-why-underdogs-win-an-astonishing-amount-of-the-time-2012-7?r=US&IR=T (archived at https://perma.cc/D97M-VB4D)

4. Simpson, J (2017) Finding brand success in the digital world, *Forbes*, 25 August, www.forbes.com/sites/forbesagencycouncil/2017/08/25/finding-brand-success-in-the-digital-world/#762e31c0626e (archived at https://perma.cc/83SA-8JNV)

5. Wikipedia (2020) Time Person of the Year, 3 October, en.wikipedia.
org/wiki/Time_Person_of_the_Year (archived at https://perma.cc/
S5TD-4CRU)

6. Wikipedia (2020) Time Person of the Year, 3 October, en.wikipedia.
org/wiki/Time_Person_of_the_Year (archived at https://perma.cc/
S5TD-4CRU)

7. National Institute of Mental Health (2018) Autism spectrum disorder,
www.nimh.nih.gov/health/publications/autism-spectrum-disorder/
index.shtml (archived at https://perma.cc/9LW9-2EZT)

8. Thunberg, G (2019) When haters go after your looks and differences,
it means they have nowhere left to go. And then you know you're
winning! I have Aspergers and that means I'm sometimes a bit
different from the norm. And – given the right circumstances – being
different is a superpower, #aspiepower [Twitter] 31 August, twitter.com/
GretaThunberg/status/1167916177927991296 (archived at
https://perma.cc/BN2K-P35G)

9. Bandura, A (1986) *Social Foundations of Thought and Action:
A social cognitive theory*, Prentice-Hall, New Jersey

10. Apple Podcasts (2020) The Skinny Confidential Him & Her Podcast
[podcast], 13 October, podcasts.apple.com/us/podcast/the-skinny-
confidential-him-her-podcast/id1093028505 (archived at
https://perma.cc/W63T-YKPN)

11. Wheeler, S (2018) The Skinny on Lauryn Evarts and The Skinny
Confidential, Influence.bloglovin.com, 13 December, influence.
bloglovin.com/the-skinny-on-lauryn-evarts-and-the-skinny-
confidential-5de09f9bfbd5 (archived at https://perma.cc/7QDE-
TQ3E)

12. Jarboe, G (2014) What 300 Hours of Video Uploaded to YouTube
Every Minute Means for Advertisers, *Tubular Insights*,
https://tubularinsights.com/300-hours-video-youtube-advertisers/
(archived at https://perma.cc/Q93Q-7YSQ)

13. Ingraham, I (2018) Leisure reading in the US is at an all-time low,
The Washington Post, 29 June, www.washingtonpost.com/gdpr-
consent/?next_url=https%3a%2f%2fwww.washingtonpost.com%2fn
ews%2fwonk%2fwp%2f2018%2f06%2f29%2fleisure-reading-in-
the-u-s-is-at-an-all-time-low%2f (archived at https://perma.cc/5Q7E-
XFE2)

14. Winn, R (2020) 2020 podcast stats & facts (new research from Oct 2020), Podcastinsights.com, 6 October, www.podcastinsights.com/podcast-statistics/ (archived at https://perma.cc/QHA4-NYM4)
15. Gray, C (2020) Podcast stats in 2020: The very latest industry facts & trends, Thepodcasthost.com, 7 May, www.thepodcasthost.com/listening/podcast-industry-stats/ (archived at https://perma.cc/4QA7-N4NV)
16. Cridland, J (2020) How the coronavirus is affecting podcast downloads, Podnews.com, 23 March, podnews.net/article/coronavirus-covid19-affecting-podcasting (archived at https://perma.cc/WK32-U7GT)

Chapter 6

1. Volpicelli, G (2017) What do you do when you've made £27m in cleaning? Get into home extensions, Wired.co.uk, 4 August, www.wired.co.uk/article/hassle-founders-alex-depledge-jules-coleman-buildpath-home-extensions (archived at https://perma.cc/L73C-HBXY)
2. Depledge, A (nd) Screw conformity: Why British entrepreneurs need to learn to be mavericks, *Management Today*, www.managementtoday.co.uk/screw-conformity-why-british-entrepreneurs-need-learn-mavericks/article/1302843 (archived at https://perma.cc/EP9P-Q599)
3. Depledge, A (nd) Screw conformity: Why British entrepreneurs need to learn to be mavericks, *Management Today*, www.managementtoday.co.uk/screw-conformity-why-british-entrepreneurs-need-learn-mavericks/article/1302843 (archived at https://perma.cc/EP9P-Q599)
4. Wallstreetmojo.com (nd) Sandbagging, www.wallstreetmojo.com/sandbagging/ (archived at https://perma.cc/426A-84J9)
5. Munro, L (2020) The half-life of your skills is shrinking, stay sharp to stay relevant, Adobe XD, 19 February, xd.adobe.com/ideas/career-tips/the-half-life-of-your-skills-is-shrinking-heres-what-you-can-do-about-it/ (archived at https://perma.cc/Z6F6-8BGD)
6. World Health Organization (2018) Ageing and health, www.who.int/news-room/fact-sheets/detail/ageing-and-health (archived at https://perma.cc/93JY-KYHS)

7. Warley, S (nd) How work is changing as you know it, Lifeskillsthatmatter.com, lifeskillsthatmatter.com/how-work-is-changing/ (archived at https://perma.cc/E23B-XU7L)

8. Credit Suisse (nd) Corporate longevity, plus.credit-suisse.com/rpc4/ravDocView?docid=V6y0SB2AF-WEr1ce (archived at https://perma.cc/W7Z8-V2VK)

9. Anthony, SD, Viguerie SP, Schwartz EI and Van Landeghem, V (2018) *2018 Corporate Longevity Forecast: Creative destruction is accelerating*, Innosight.com, www.innosight.com/insight/creative-destruction/ (archived at https://perma.cc/QC9C-KPYD)

10. Shah, D (2018) By the numbers: MOOCs in 2018, Classcentral.com, 11 December, www.classcentral.com/report/mooc-stats-2018/ (archived at https://perma.cc/86ZH-BFV7)

11. Rework:withgoogle.com (nd) Re:Work, Tool: Grade OKRs, rework.withgoogle.com/guides/set-goals-with-okrs/steps/grade-OKRs/ (archived at https://perma.cc/V5UE-2MNS)

12. Doerr, J (2018) *Measure What Matters: How Google, Bono, and the Gates Foundation rock the world with OKRs*, Penguin, New York

Chapter 7

1. Fricke, D (2012) Jimmy Iovine: The man with the magic ears, *Rolling Stone*, 12 April, www.rollingstone.com/music/music-news/jimmy-iovine-the-man-with-the-magic-ears-120618/ (archived at https://perma.cc/E5G3-3BNQ)

2. Fricke, D (2012) Jimmy Iovine: The man with the magic ears, *Rolling Stone*, 12 April, www.rollingstone.com/music/music-news/jimmy-iovine-the-man-with-the-magic-ears-120618/ (archived at https://perma.cc/E5G3-3BNQ)

3. *The Defiant Ones*, Allen Hughes, dir. (HBO, 2017) [film]

4. Hainey, M (2014) The music legend who just might save Apple, *GQ*, 13 November, www.gq.com/story/jimmy-iovine-men-of-the-year-icon (archived at https://perma.cc/T4DC-5GA4)

5. *The Defiant Ones*, Allen Hughes, dir. (HBO, 2017) [film]

6. Brueck, H and Gal, S (2020) How the coronavirus death toll compares to other pandemics, including SARS, HIV, and the Black Death, *Business Insider*, 22 May, www.businessinsider.com/

coronavirus-deaths-how-pandemic-compares-to-other-deadly-
outbreaks-2020-4?r=US&IR=T (archived at https://perma.cc/
YNJ2-YHUV)

7. Apple (nd) Privacy-preserving contact tracing, press release, covid19.
apple.com/contacttracing (archived at https://perma.cc/DC7L-E4YE)

8. Hersko, T (2019) Analysis: Quibi continues to excite investors despite
experimental design, Indiewire.com, 9 July, www.indiewire.com/
2019/07/quibi-investor-analysis-1202156711/ (archived at
https://perma.cc/EJY7-KNCF)

9. *Wall Street Journal* (2020) Quibi is shutting down barely six months
after going live, www.wsj.com/articles/quibi-weighs-shutting-down-
as-problems-mount-11603301946 (archived at https://perma.cc/
NWE2-GNU4)

10. Sperling, N (2020) Jeffrey Katzenberg blames pandemic for Quibi's
rough start, *The New York Times*, www.nytimes.com/2020/05/11/
business/media/jeffrey-katzenberg-quibi-coronavirus.html (archived
at https://perma.cc/W5FV-NY2Q)

11. Spangler, T (2018) Jeffrey Katzenberg's NewTV startup closes $1
billion, all major studios among investors, *Variety*, 7 August, variety.
com/2018/digital/news/newtv-jeffrey-katzenberg-meg-whitman-1-
billion-funding-1202897529/ (archived at https://perma.cc/WNT4-
ZLAZ)

12. Bloom, D (2019) Quibi by the numbers: Does it add up to a new tv
paradigm? Tvrev.com, 10 June, tvrev.com/quibi-by-the-numbers-does-
it-add-up-to-a-new-tv-paradigm/ (archived at https://perma.cc/5L9R-
78L6)

13. Rivera, LA (2012) Hiring as cultural matching: The case of elite
professional service firms, *American Sociological Review*,
28 November, journals.sagepub.com/doi/10.1177/
0003122412463213 (archived at https://perma.cc/VHV9-VHV7)

14. Farrell, PE (2014) The 7 deadly sins of joint ventures, *Entrepreneur
Europe*, 2 September, www.entrepreneur.com/article/236987#:~:text=
It's%20estimated%20at%20least%2040,percent%2C%20of%20
joint%20ventures%20fail.&text=Successful%20joint%20
ventures%20can%20offer,property%20rights%20are%20at%20risk
(archived at https://perma.cc/GU9J-49L7)

15. Marzarotto, M (2018) The evolution of music festivals and the power
of an experience, Medium.com, 20 November, medium.com/

@malu_14611/the-evolution-of-music-festivals-and-the-power-of-an-experience-f98be2b9a5c1 (archived at https://perma.cc/WU65-47WF)

16. Garcia, L-M (2014) A pre-history of the electronic music festival, Residentadvisor.net, 14 July, www.residentadvisor.net/features/2104 (archived at https://perma.cc/BKL7-9ZKW)

17. Instagram (nd) '#cochella' online, www.instagram.com/explore/tags/coachella/?hl=en (archived at https://perma.cc/ELY9-DCWC)

18. Eventbrite (2014) Millennials: Fueling the experience economy, eventbrite-s3.s3.amazonaws.com/marketing/Millennials_Research/Gen_PR_Final.pdf (archived at https://perma.cc/GFX4-W42C)

19. Gajanan, M (2019) How music festivals became a massive business in the 50 years since Woodstock, *Time*, 14 August, time.com/5651255/business-of-music-festivals/ (archived at https://perma.cc/R8WX-ML3Q)

20. Interview with Rebecca Jolly

21. *Rolling Stone* (1999) Performance: Coachella Music and Arts Festival, 5 November

22. Huddleston, T (2019) Fyre Festival: How a 25-year-old scammed investors out of $26 million, CNBC, 18 August, www.cnbc.com/2019/08/18/how-fyre-festivals-organizer-scammed-investors-out-of-26-million.html (archived at https://perma.cc/F7XP-KNX7)

23. Baggs, M (2019) Fyre Festival: Inside the world's biggest festival flop, BBC News, 18 January, www.bbc.co.uk/news/newsbeat-46904445 (archived at https://perma.cc/58GK-KXRV)

24. Swant, M (2019) Ja Rule talks about marketing Fyre Festival and if it might happen again, *Forbes*, 15 November, www.forbes.com/sites/martyswant/2019/11/15/ja-rule-talks-about-marketing-fyre-festival-and-if-it-might-happen-again/#73d204b5416b (archived at https://perma.cc/2WM9-PYWW)

25. Bluestone, G (2019) Ja Rule said Fyre Festival's celebrity-packed marketing targeted 'kids that grew up socially awkward, not the A crowd', *Insider*, 15 November, www.insider.com/ja-rule-fyre-fest-was-for-socially-awkward-kids-not-a-crowd-2019-11 (archived at https://perma.cc/3N5W-UCE2)

26. McLaren (2015) Case study: GSK, www.mclaren.com/group/case-studies/case-study-gsk/ (archived at https://perma.cc/HH8Z-CYWS)

Chapter 8

1. Lee, A (2013) Welcome to the Unicorn Club: Learning from billion-dollar startups, techcrunch.com, 2 November, techcrunch.com/2013/11/02/welcome-to-the-unicorn-club/?guccounter=1 (archived at https://perma.cc/NM47-47YE)
2. Denning, T (2017) What I learned from the world's greatest venture capitalist, Entrepreneur.com, 3 April, www.entrepreneur.com/article/287525 (archived at https://perma.cc/K523-HBN6)
3. Interview with Bill Tai
4. Wilding, M (2018) How Wetherspoon's conquered Britain, *Esquire*, 3 July, www.esquire.com/uk/food-drink/a19129642/how-wetherspoons-conquered-britain/ (archived at https://perma.cc/445C-HGW6)
5. Office for National Statistics (2018) Adult drinking habits in Great Britain: 2017, www.ons.gov.uk/peoplepopulationandcommunity/healthandsocialcare/drugusealcoholandsmoking/bulletins/opinionsandlifestylesurveyadultdrinkinghabitsingreatbritain/2017 (archived at https://perma.cc/WPP7-DRER)
6. Farrell, S (2019) Wetherspoons shareholders call time on pro-Brexit politics in pubs, *The Guardian*, 10 November, www.theguardian.com/business/2019/nov/10/wetherspoon-tim-martin-brexit-leave-agm-corporate-governance (archived at https://perma.cc/Q9A4-LMUK)
7. BBC (2018) Trump: NFL kneelers 'maybe shouldn't be in country', BBC News, 24 May, www.bbc.co.uk/news/world-us-canada-44232979 (archived at https://perma.cc/63P9-UDNV)
8. Beer, J (2019) One year later, what did we learn from Nike's blockbuster Colin Kaepernick ad? Fast Company, 9 May, www.fastcompany.com/90399316/one-year-later-what-did-we-learn-from-nikes-blockbuster-colin-kaepernick-ad (archived at https://perma.cc/24HD-LCZ6)
9. Cadogan, D (2019) MyBeautyBrand is the new platform promising to be the influencer antidote, Dazeddigital.com, 28 November, www.dazeddigital.com/beauty/head/article/46952/1/my-beauty-brand-launch-robin-derrick-interview-make-up-nails-new-platform (archived at https://perma.cc/QQF5-W6N2)

10. March, B (2019) MyBeautyBrand is like a digital Avon for Gen Zers, *Harper's Bazaar*, https://www.harpersbazaar.com/uk/beauty/ a30073258/mybeautybrand/ (archived at https://perma.cc/62SV-UW7J)

11. Lutke, T (2020) As of today, Shopify is a digital by default company. We will keep our offices closed until 2021 so that we can rework them for this new reality. And after that, most will permanently work remotely. Office centricity is over, [Twitter] 21 May, twitter.com/tobi/ status/1263483496087064579 (archived at https://perma.cc/858L-QDLB)

12. KPMG (2020) KPMG 2020 CEO outlook: COVID-19 Special Edition, home.kpmg/xx/en/home/insights/2020/08/global-ceo-outlook-2020.html (archived at https://perma.cc/NV6W-CVAG)

13. Interview with Mark Mylam

Index

NB: page numbers in *italic* indicate figures or tables

#MeToo movement 52, 63

5G technology 61
21st Century Fox 165

Accenture 140
active learning 148
advice, taking 83–84
Alba, Jessica 126
Amazon 3, 71, 72
    Amazon Employees for Climate
        Justice 64, 65–66, 74
Android 164
Apple 157, 163
    Beats by Dre 3, 160, 161, 175
    Beats Music 160
Apprentice, The 133–36, 138–39
assets, business 35, 39, 185
authenticity 122–26
    communication management 124
    consistency 123
    'on brand', being 125–26
    rewarding 192–93
    trolling, dealing with 125
Avon 42

Baby Boomers 76, 77, 95, 96
Baldwin, Hailey 172
Bandura, Albert 122, 124
*Be More Pirate or How to Take on the
    World and Win* 26
Beastie Boys 34
Beats by Dre 3, 160, 161, 175
Beats Music 160
Beyoncé 172
Bezos, Jeff 65, 66, 120
Black Lives Matter movement 52, 76,
    190
blogging 148
Bloomberg West TV 92–93
Bosstick, Lauryn Evarts 125–26

Brailsford, Dave 17–18, 33, 98, 121
Brand, Stewart 53–56, 57, 58, 66, 72,
    78, 127
Branson, Richard 19, 30, 33, 34
BrewDog 81–84, 119–20
    advice, taking 83–84
    Equity for Punks 104
    industry awards, winning 82
Brexit 56, 57, 188–89
Bre-X Minerals 35
*Business for Punks: Break all the rules
    – the BrewDog way* 82–83
Butler, Gerard 13

Cambridge Analytica 59
Candy Crush 57
Carter, Jimmy 120
CEO exits 48
change, positive 89–91
'cheerleaders' 168
Clean Air Act 60
climate change 1
Clinton, Hillary 62
Coachella 169–70, 171–72
co-creation 160
Code for America 152
cognitive dissonance 90
collaboration
    advice, taking 162
    choosing collaborators 167–68
    co-creation 160
    collaborative leadership 95–98
    complacency 174–76
    long-term partnerships, building
        176–77
    OKRs, individual 178
    skill sets, complementary 177–78
    traditional businesses 161
    trust, importance of 178
    vs influencer marketing 161
    with competitors 163–64

communication management 124
Conniff Allende, Sam 26
conspiracy theories 61–62
Covid-19 pandemic 1, 20
   conspiracy theories 61, 62
   partnerships 162–64
   podcasting 130
   Quibi 165
   remote working 70, 94, 194–95
   Saudi Aramco, effect on 16
   work culture 74
Cramer, Jim 91

Dairy Queen 21
Daisley, Bruce 73, 74, 77
d'Ancona, Matthew 61, 62, 77
David and Goliath 113
Defiant Ones, The 159
Degas, Edgar 169
democracy 1, 22
Depledge, Alex 140, 162
Derrick, Robin 192–93
Dickie, Martin 82
Direct Marketing Association 24
direct-to-consumer 42, 46–47
Disney 43–44, 165
Duckworth, Angela 113, 114, 125
Dunbar, Robin 100–01, 169
Dutch East India Company 14–16,
   19

Eat Sleep Work Repeat 74
e-commerce 36
   direct-to-consumer 42, 46–47
ELLE UK 46
Entertainment One 165
Equity for Punks 104
Evaluate a Job Offer Study 76
experiences, creating 19
expertise, gaining 127–30
   engaging 130
   listening 129–30
   task batching 128–29
Extreme Tech Challenge 29–32, 33–35

Facebook 41, 43, 92, 100, 140
   Coachella 171
   Google walkout, impact of 64
   launch of 22, 57

   political advertising 62
   Tomorrowland 171
failure, fear of 137–38, 143
fake news 61
Fenty Beauty 37–38, 71
Fiorina, Carly 92
First Industrial Revolution 182
Forbes 3, 43
Fourth Industrial Revolution 183
Fuller, Buckminster 54
Fyre Festival 3, 172–76
   experience, lack of 174–75
   legal fallout 173
   promotion of 172–73

Galton, Jane 150
Gandhi, Mahatma 120
Gates, Bill 92
gender inequality 1
General Assembly 149
Generation X 76, 89, 95, 96
Generation Z 93
gig economy, the 68–71, 191
   equal pay 69–70
   Millennials 70
   size of 68
   tech, role of 68–69
Gilbert, Rhod 138
Gladwell, Malcolm 113–14
GlaxoSmithKline (GSK) 179–80
Global Millennial Survey 2019 75
goal-setting 150–54
   implementation 153–54
   OKRs (Objectives and Key
      Results) 151–53
   SMART goals 150–51
Gold 35
'golden circle' theory 76
Google 92
   Apple partnership 163
   Google Alerts 128
   launch of 22, 57
   OKRs 151, 153
   walkout 63–64, 71, 72
Great British Entrepreneur Awards 25
Great Hack, The 59
Great Recession 67–68
'greatness', entrepreneurial 17
grit, importance of 113, 114

*Grit: The power of passion and
    perseverance* 113

Hadid, Bella 172
Hanks, Tom 61
Harrods 106
Hassle 140, 161
HubSpot 147
Huffington Post 91
Hyman, Louis 68

ice wine 107
influencers 43–44, 161, 171
    'influencer fatigue' 192–93
    vs collaboration 161
Information Commissioner's Office 59
Instagram 66, 125
    Coachella 170
    Fyre Festival 172
    influencers 43
    'Insta-famous' 2
    Jenner, Kylie 139
    M.92 45–46
Intel 152
internet, the 22, 51
Interscope 157
iOS 164
Iovine, Jimmy 157–60, 175, 176
iPhone 57
ITV 165

Jackson, Michael 82, 84
Ja Rule 172–76, 178
JD Wetherspoon 187–89
Jenner, Kendall 172
Jenner, Kylie 48, 71, 161, 176
    authenticity 39, 41–42, 191
    experience, need for 72
    Instagram 45, 139
    Keeping Up with the Kardashians
        38
    job security 67–70, 97
    Great Recession 67, 68
Jobs, Steve 56, 92
Johnson, Cory 91–93
Jolly, Rebecca 171–72, 173
Jordan, Michael 92
Joy of Work, The 74
Joy's Law 71

Kaepernick, Colin 189–90
Katzenberg, Jeffrey 165
Keeping Up with the Kardashians 38
Kennedy, John F 55
King Jr, Martin Luther 120
Kloss, Karlie 124
Knight, Phil 190
Kylie Cosmetics 3, 38–39, 41, 72, 192

Lehman Brothers 67
LinkedIn 93, 148, 152
Lionsgate 165
Littner, Claude 138
L'Oréal 37–38, 39, 47, 147
LVMH 37, 71

M.92 44–45, 46, 47, 48, 176
Major League Baseball 190
Major League Soccer 190
Maker Studios 43–44
*Making the Most of Being Mentored:
    How to grow from a
    mentoring partnership* 87
Mamilova, Maryam and Amina 45,
    46
Markoff, John 56
Martin, Tim 187–89
Maslow, Abraham 59
McConaughey, Matthew 35
McFarland, Billy 172–76, 178
McLaren Automotive Group 179–80
McNamee, Roger 103
Media Week 24
Mentee's Guide, The 87
*Mentee's Guide: How to have a
    successful relationship with
    a mentor* 87
mentorship 86–87
MGM 165
Microsoft 64
Millennials 88–89
    collaborative leadership 96
    diversity 76
    festivals and events 169, 170
    gig economy, the 70
    Great Recession 67
    positive change 89
    purpose, desire for 75
    remote working 93

social media 89
trust in the media 75
values and business 76
mindset, changing your 13
mission statements 119
Monster Cable Products 160, 175
Motorola 152
Murray, Daisy 46
Musk, Elon 33, 87, 92
MyBeautyBrand 192–93
Mylam, Mark
    first weeks 22–23
    future leader, as a 193–95
    hiring 10–11
    interviewing 8

Napster 100
NASA 55
National Basketball Association 190
National Hockey League 190
NBCUniversal 165
Necker Island 29–32, 33–35, 39
Negroponte, Nicholas 51
Netflix 58, 152
networking, importance of 22, 84–85
Neumann, Adam 103
neuro-linguistic programming (NLP)
    13
NFL 189
    NFL Regional Combines 142–43,
    145
Nicks, Stevie 157
Nike 189–90
N.W.A. 158

Obama, Barack 62
Ocasio-Cortez, Alexandria 62–63
OKRs (Objectives and Key Results)
    151–53
    individual 178
Old Wives' Tales 60
'on brand', being 125–26
online courses 148–49
originality, importance of 17
oversharing 98–99

Page, Larry 153
Parker, Sean 100

passion, following your 112–18
    abilities, your 116–17
    activities, favourite 116
    grit, importance of 113, 114
    prioritizing 117–18
    underdogs 113–14
    values, your 115, 116
patterns, learning through 12–14
PayPal 33, 45
Peet, Alfred 18
Picnic Ventures 101
pirates, as rebels 26
Pirc 188
podcasts 130
population, global 12, 146
'post-truth' 58–59
Post-Truth: The New War on Truth
    and How to Fight Back 61
Prince 24
Pursuit of Happiness 17

QAnon 61
Quibi 164–67
    collaborative model 165–67
    Covid-19, impact of 165

race inequality 1, 94–95
Ratajkowski, Emily 172
REBEL Pi Ice Wine 83, 108–09
Red Bull 24
Resi 140, 161
Rihanna 37, 48, 71
Rivera, Lauren 168
Robbins, Tony 13
Rolling Stone 158

sandbagging 141–45
Saud, Fahad 98–99, 100, 101
Saudi Aramco 16
Second Industrial Revolution 182–83
Seed Beauty 38–39, 71, 161, 176
sexual harassment 1
Shakur, Tupac 158
Shopify 45, 195
Shultz, Howard 18–19
Siebel, Tom 93
Siegl, Zev, Bowker, Gordon and
    Baldwin, Jerry 18